·52·

CREATIVE

family time

EXPERIENCES

FUN WAYS TO BRING FAITH HOME

Timothy Smith

randall house
114 Bush Rd | Nashville, TN 37217 | randallhouse.com

Table of Contents

PART THREE: Milestones Moments: Rites of Passage & Holidays

iv

•Part One•

INFORMAL MOMENTS

Introduction

"It's *epic* out there!" said my friend Tom as he shook the water from his ears and set his surfboard on the grass at The Point in Ventura. The northwest winter swell brought frigid water temperatures and an eight-foot swell. "I caught a right all the way from *Stables* to past the *Point!* Yeah, it was *epic!*"

Epic—We surfers use the word, but only to describe conditions, waves, and experiences that are worth talking about. We call it "talking story." It's the surf culture's narrative tradition. In the evenings, as we gather, we swap stories about the day: who caught the best wave, who had the worst wipe-out, who did the most-lame thing on land, etc. But only the biggest and best stories are reserved for the adjective—*epic*.

As I thought about talking story, it occurred to me that this was exactly what God wants us to do with our children at home and as we walk on the way with them. Take time to talk about HIS story. God's story is epic!

Your kids are Generation iY—the younger half of a generation highly influenced by the Internet, iTunes, iPhones, instant info, and the immediate reward of moving up a level in a video game, or instantly ordering their urge *du jour* online. All of these "I"s add up to a very "I-centered" child.

Engaging our children, especially around spiritual issues and topics, can't be done in a lecture. I like what Dr. Tim Elmore writes in his book *Generation iY—Our Last Chance to Save Their Future.* [1]

A lecture isn't enough anymore—or at least we cannot *begin* with a lecture. If we want to be heard, we must engage iYers' interest with an experience that captures their imagination. They want to do or see something. They want action and interaction. So instead of asking, "What do I want to say?" we should ask ourselves, "How can I say it creatively and experientially?"

I would add, "How can we learn to ask questions instead of lecture?" Gen iY is more likely to respond to *talking story* and having a conversation than a lecture—especially preteens and teens. Recent research on what makes faith stick with adolescents and young adults supports this. Researchers and authors, Drs. Kara E. Powell and Chap Clark write:

> Throughout our research process, parents have repeatedly told us that their best conversations with their kids occur in the midst of everyday life—when they are in the minivan together talking about soccer practice, or when their kid is stressed over finding a prom date. Those times of crisis or debriefings of the day's events are often the best springboards for deeper conversations . . . One of the most important pieces of *Sticky Faith* communication advice we can share is this: **never explain something to your kid if you can ask a question instead.**[2]

The Bible expects parents to be the primary influencers of spiritual formation with their children, with the church and other ministries in a supportive role. But what does it mean to be a "spiritual leader" in the home? Do we have to light candles? Have organ music playing? Sing Gregorian chants? How can we as parents influence our Gen iY children?

The good news is that **parents are usually the most important influence** in their children's lives. Dr. Christian Smith, from the University of Notre Dame found, in a survey of more than three thousand teens and their parents that the most important social influence in shaping young people's religious lives is the religious life modeled and taught to them by their parents.[3] He

4

also said, on a panel that I heard, "When it comes to kid's faith, parents get what *they* are."[4]

You get what you are. What are your kids picking up from your passion and example? What are you passing on to your kids? Are you talking story? Are you talking about God's story, or are you outsourcing spiritual growth to the church, the youth group, or the Christian school?

So how do we connect in an *epic* way with our kids? Remember that this generation wants an experience before an explanation. Futurist Leonard Sweet describes today's culture and Gen iY as **EPIC—Experiential, Participatory, Image-rich and Connected.**[5]

- **Experiential**—Our kids want to engage their senses to see, touch or do something, not simply *hear* about it.

- **Participatory**—Gen iY wants to express themselves online, with Tweets, *Facebook* posts, and texting their votes for their favorite on the singing and dance competition shows on TV.

- **Image-rich**—Spending nearly eight hours a day in front of a screen, this is a visually oriented crew. Images, icons, and brands may be their language more than words.

- **Connected**—Teens don't see their phone as a tool as much as an appendage. It is always with them and they "need" it to stay connected with their friends and the emerging news and social events.

52 Creative Family Time Experiences is designed to set up three kinds of *epic* moments with your kids:

1. **Informal**—daily moments when you can impress faith.

2. **Intentional family times**—that you schedule weekly, or every other week.

3. **Milestones**—holidays and rites of passage when you affirm spiritual growth.

My hope and prayer is that you would strategically and intentionally plan epic conversations and experiences with your children that generate experiencing God together. Don't worry about doing it perfectly. Sometimes the failures and flubs make the biggest impressions. Something is better than nothing. Apply grace where needed.

Enjoy the epic journey,

Timothy Smith
www.ParentsCoach.org

Peanut Butter Families

What is it about peanut butter that makes it so popular? Most homes in North America always have a jar in the cupboard. I think peanut butter is so popular because it is tasty, nutritious, easy-to-use, and affordable. But one characteristic about peanut butter stands out—it's sticky. Just for fun, watch a *You Tube®* video of a dog eating peanut butter. It's hilarious! In fact, watch it with your kids.

What would happen in our families if we had *peanut butter faith*—tasty, nutritious, simple, and sticky?

Did you know that at least fifty percent of the children who are active in their faith and church involvement stop being involved as older teens or in their college years? What made the difference for the minority of kids who retained their faith? What made their faith *sticky?*

One of the factors for the young people who retained their faith was that they talked about faith at home. I think the problem is that parents have *outsourced* spiritual formation to the church or the Christian school. The solution is for Christian parents to become the *primary trainers* of spiritual formation for their children and teens, and have the church serve a *secondary* and supportive role.

Of course, the issue is that most parents don't know how to do this. But that is the purpose of *52 Creative Family Time Experiences*—to train parents to have formal and informal conversations and experiences with their children about faith.

Talking about faith at home is very biblical:

Write these commandments that I've given you today on your hearts. Get them inside of you and then get them inside your children. Talk about them wherever you are sitting at home or walking in the street, talk about them from the time you get up in the morning to when you fall into bed at night. Tie them on your hands and foreheads as a reminder. Inscribe them on the doorposts of your homes and on your city gates. (Deuteronomy 6:5–9, *The Message*)

This Scripture is a portion of *The Shema*—the most quoted Scripture and repeated prayer in the world. Observant Jews are likely to recite it six or more times daily. It's God's pathway for spiritual formation in the home. So it's a good place for us to start. It provides a template for informal faith talks.

Ideally, you will have a combination of formal and informal faith talks with your kids. The formal talks often set up the informal. But some families never have formal family times, but they are still peanut butter families—with sticky faith. How did they do it?

MAKING PEANUT BUTTER FAITH

According to *The Shema*, as parents we should impress God's Word on our hearts first: "Get them inside of you, and then get them inside of your children." We can't impress on our child's heart something we don't have on our own.

The disconnect for many well-meaning Christian parents, is this essential first step. They skip the self-impression stage and jump right to the child-impression stage, and the child notices the disconnect between what a parent says and what he lives.

We talk about what our heart is set on. Our passions are reflected in our conversations. If God's Word has impressed our hearts, we can't help but talk about Him and His word.

According to *The Shema*, there are four opportunities for natural faith talks with our kids:

- *Talk as you **sit** at home*
- ***Walk** and talk on the way*
- *When you **get up***
- *When you **lie down***

TALK AS YOU SIT AT HOME

- **Dining room**—Do you pray at meals? 90% of Christian families only pray at meals. Do you weave spiritual topics into your mealtime conversations?
- **Living room**—Do you read the Bible and Christian books together?
- **Family room**—Do you plan intentional family times together (like the ideas in this book?) Have you set guidelines for media?
- **Office**—Do you protect yourself and kids from harmful content from the Internet? Do you limit online time so you and your kids have real face time for talking?

To talk at home, you have to be home, you have to be available, approachable, and ready to focus on your children and what is of lasting significance.

WALK AND TALK ON THE WAY

Let's face it—we don't do a lot of "walking in the street" even though most of us could use it. We are more likely to be "driving in the SUV" with our kids. Either way, it's time we have that we can leverage for spiritual formation with our children. I'm not saying we have to spiritualize everything, but we can use the natural conversations of the day to point out supernatural and spiritual truths. I call this the *Walk and Talk Strategy*—when we weave spiritual insights into normal conversations as we walk or drive.

"Look at that beautiful tree. I'm so glad God made trees. They help clean the air, give birds a place to live and they are pretty to look at. Thank God for trees! What do you like about trees?" (This example is directed towards a preschooler, not a high school student, unless you want to see their eyes roll.)

For many parents the *Walk and Talk Strategy* is a good place to start. You might start here and work up to having a family time. To create the right atmosphere in the car, you might need to turn off the video, radio, or texting for the drive so you can create space to talk. I know parents of teens who have a "no text policy" on one way to school—either in the morning or going home in the afternoon, so they have a few minutes to connect. Other parents set a "no text—let's talk" zone for part of the drive.

WHEN YOU GET UP

I can hear what you are thinking, "Talk about faith in the mornings? When everyone is grumpy and rushed!" Our family is normal. Mornings are difficult for us too. Especially for me until I've had my coffee! We don't have a lot of time, so we have discovered that as we grab a quick bowl of cereal or toast, we asked each other, "How can I pray for you today?" My daughter might say, "I have a test today." Or my wife, a middle school teacher, might say, "I give a test today. Pray that my students remember what I taught them." We start the day asking, *I wonder where we will see God at work today?* It's common for us to part saying, "I love you. Praying for you."

WHEN YOU LIE DOWN

I like *The Message* paraphrase of *The Shema:* "when you *fall* into bed at night." [Emphasis added]. As parents, we are so exhausted at night that we fall into bed.

Hopefully, before we nod off, we can tuck our kids into bed, pray with them, read them a story and ask, "Where did you see God at work today?" or "How did you do on the test?"

You can also read your child stories from the Bible or an illustrated Bible storybook. Ask, "What does this story teach us about God?" Emphasize the character and attributes of God more than the hero in the story. Our goal is to reinforce that God is always the same–yesterday, today, and forever. He is always good. He is always with you. This is what we call the meta-narrative or God's Big Story. Reflecting on God, His qualities, and unchanging promises at bedtime reassures and comforts your child, regardless of her age.

WHEREVER—WHENEVER

God's plan for faith at home is wherever and whenever. It's a **lifestyle**. Mastering any skill requires practice and repetition. I have met parents who say, "We tried doing family times or having faith talks, but our kids didn't like it, so we stopped."

The mother of all learning is repetition. Let's say you sign your daughter up to play soccer. She gets her uniform, the cleats, the shin guards, and loves going to practice and the first few games, where you stand in cold, drizzly weather on Saturdays, hoping she will kick the ball in the right direction! The next week, she complains to you that she doesn't want to go to practice, can't find her other cleat and wants to quit the team.

What would you do?

I'd say, "You aren't quitting. We paid the money. You are on the team. You will finish the season. Now put on your jersey and get in the van. If you only have one soccer shoe, you will have to hop all over the field on one leg!"

Most of us would say something like that. We know the repetition and practice is good for her. We would make her do things she doesn't want to do and isn't *comfortable* with because we know they are good for her.

Sports are good, but spiritual formation is better. Be disciplined at it. Work at it. Don't quit at the first sign of resistance.

Here's a riddle: if *repetition is the mother of all learning,* who or what is the father?

According to *The Shema,* the father of all learning is **sensational**—using all five senses to remind yourself and your children of God and His promises. You may have heard of learning languages or learning modalities. Everyone has a preferred learning style. Our Creator shaped us to learn in different ways. Some learn best with their hands. Others learn best with visual input. Still others learn best from conversation.

"Tie them on your hands and foreheads as a reminder; inscribe them on the doorposts of your homes and on your city gates." (Deuteronomy 6:8-9)

- **TOUCH**—tactile learners can "tie" something on their wrists to remember spiritual truth.

- **VISUAL**—visual learners can see the symbol on the doorpost and be reminded of God's promises. Some homes feature a favorite Scripture by the doorway. This is called a Mezuzah. The doorposts signify the coming and going of life. Spiritual formation is part of our daily routine as we go through the doorway. Doorposts will sometimes have pencil marks on them to measure our child's height, and recording their physical growth. But doorways can also represent spiritual growth: "Remember when you walked out this door and went to summer camp and made a spiritual commitment?"

- **VERBAL**—Consider inscribing Scripture and important words somewhere in your home. We painted our family mission statement above the door in large letters: *Grace sees beauty in everything.*

- **AUDITORY**—Music can help some children retain spiritual truth. Positive words of blessing have a huge impact. Both of these are auditory. Quote *The Shema* or other Scriptures of blessing to your child (Zephaniah 3:17). Words of affirmation help your child feel secure, loved, accepted, and valuable.

- **SMELL**—Several times in Scripture fragrance is mentioned (2 Corinthians 2:15–16). The most powerful, memory-enhancing sense is our sense of smell. That's why a waft of perfume from a passerby can take us back to a decade-old memory. Consider ways to use candles, spices, aromas, and food to create a fragrant memory. Jesus engaged the senses of His disciples at the Last Supper, "This do in remembrance of me." Smell the fresh-baked bread. Remember the waft of the wine; causing us to reflect on His sacrifice.

- **TASTE**—I think it's interesting that at pivotal times in Scripture food is involved. In the garden, it was the forbidden fruit. In the Exodus, it was manna. Canaan was known for its milk and honey. Food is our sustenance. Jesus is the Bread of life. Again, at His Last Supper, Jesus chooses to use food and the human sense of taste to drive home a profound spiritual truth. Can we use food for spiritual purposes?

As I said previously, this book is your guide for **three kinds of moments:**

1. **Informal,** daily moments when you can impress faith.

2. Intentional **family times** that you schedule weekly, or every other week.

3. **Milestones:** holidays and rites of passage when you affirm spiritual growth.

These moments don't happen by accident. You have to take the time. You have to make a plan. You need to start small. Why not start today?

Take a look at the *Family Faith Plan* on pages 16-17. It provides **thirty-six impression points** for parents to talk about and model faith in the natural flow of our family life. As you can see, the plan is based on the flow of *The Shema*. What can *you* do to impress God's commandments on yourself first? Then how might you do it as you talk with your child as you sit at home? As you walk and drive along the way? How will you impress faith in the hurried morning hours? How might you use dinner, evenings, and bedtimes to have faith conversations?

Children and adults learn best in different ways. The *Family Faith Plan* lists six learning languages (modalities) for you to consider for your children. Typically, every family is multi-lingual when it comes to learning. You have more than one kind of learning language. You may find it easy to talk with your son and use verbal instructions, but his learning language might be more tactile and hands-on. He might require more touch, physical training, and modeling. Instead of telling him how to rake leaves, you show him how to hold the rake, how to pull it along the lawn, how to grab the pile, and put it into the recycler. When it comes to training him for spiritual truth, you will need to take a more physical training approach than simply talking. But with your daughter, who has the same learning language as you, you may be able to simple talk with her.

Learning a foreign language isn't easy; it requires determination, practice, and persistence. But families that intentionally seek to impress faith and have a plan to do so are significantly more successful at passing along lasting faith to their children.

Language has a huge influence on culture. If we talk about faith in our children's learning languages, they will be more likely to embrace the culture of a Christ-centered home. They will be more likely to embrace Christ.

FAMILY FAITH PLAN:

Senses	You	Talk	Walk
Touch	Thank God for my health	Sit close when we talk	Hold hands on walk
Visual	"I wonder where I will see God at work today."	"I see a pretty bird."	"Let's look for something we like that God made."
Verbal	"Thank God for a new day!"	Listen and talk	"Thank God we are healthy enough to walk."
Hear	Read a Psalm of praise out loud	Listen to podcast	Pray for the injured when you hear sirens
Smell	Thank God for Coffee!	Bake cookies together	Stop and thank God for the smell of roses
Taste	Thank God at each meal & snack	Eat the cookies!	Count how many places you have to eat at as you drive

PEANUT BUTTER FAMILIES

36 Impression Points

AM	PM	SYMBOLS
Hug your child	Kiss your child	Sign of the Cross on their forehead
Compliment Your child's hair, choice of clothes, etc.	"Where did you see God show up today?"	Make a Mezuzah for your front door.
"I will be praying for you today as you take that test."	"I prayed for your test today. How did it go?"	Write prayer or note of encouragement and put in lunch.
Play positive, upbeat music as you get ready	Play soothing, calming praise music	Applause for kind words or actions
"Your hair smells terrific!"	Bubble bath with fragrance	Light a fragrant candle. Attach a spiritual significance with it.
"Thank you God for my tasty breakfast."	"After we read the Bible story we will have dessert."	Surprise your child with random Hershey Kisses with notes, "I love you— praying 4 u."

I suggest starting with impressing God's Word on *your* heart, then trying to get a "small win" of one of these thirty-six impression points. You can change them to fit your style, personality, pace, and child. But make them small, easy, and quick. That will give you the confidence to try more. Before you know it, you will have a lifestyle of faith formation.

Here's how a few parents used *The Family Faith Plan:*

"I was nervous about going to the parenting seminar because I knew that we weren't doing anything at home except praying over meals. I knew there had to be more, but I wasn't sure what, or how to do it. I didn't grow up in a Christian home, so I'm not sure how to grow faith in kids. At work, we have plans and goals, so having this matrix made sense to me. I liked the option of designing something that fits our family. Now, on Saturdays, I'm hiking with my son and talking about God's beautiful creation. We have a blank book we call our 'Trail Book' that records the trails, the plants, animals, and vistas we see and our prayers. I didn't know faith at home could be that much fun."

—EDGAR, ANNAPOLIS, MD

"My kids rush off to middle school and high school in the morning. It's all I can do to get them a bagel and a piece of fruit before they have to catch the bus. I want them to remember God and feel loved, so I text them a short Scripture or prayer that they can read on the bus. It takes twenty seconds, but they tell me it sets a positive tone for the day."

—ISABELLA, NEW CANAAN, CT

"Each of us plays a musical instrument. We have invested thousands in lessons and instruments and band fees over the years. After hearing you present the Family Faith Plan, we decided to do a weekly family worship concert. We sing and play together for

three or four songs, then pray. It takes less than twenty minutes, but it's the highlight of our week. Our kids look forward to it, even the teenager!"

—MICHAEL, DENVER, CO

"My kids and I love to watch all the cooking shows on TV and cook. My husband and I discussed how we could use the **Family Faith Plan** *to use taste, smell, and touch to engage our children (ages 8, 11 & 14) in something they all enjoy—cooking and eating! We are finding it easy to work in faith talks as we cook together."*

—LORI, LANSING, MI

How might you make an impression on your child? Use the blank **Family Faith Plan** to design a custom plan that fits your kids' unique needs and learning styles.

FAMILY FAITH PLAN:

Senses	YOU	TALK	WALK
Touch			
Visual			
Verbal			
Hear			
Smell			
Taste			

36 Impression Points

AM	PM	SYMBOLS

If you combine your customized thirty-six informal *impression points* with the fifty-two *intentional* family times (in the next section), you will **have eighty-eight EPIC moments** to impress faith and love on your children. Eighty-eight EPIC connections in one year! Can you imagine the impact?

•Part Two•

INTENTIONAL MOMENTS

Starting Out:

FAMILY TIME EXPERIENCES

Ever promise your children you'd take them to an amusement park? They may be excited for days—until you get there! Then as they gaze up at the roller coaster, or the spinning gizmo, or the animal-shaped car that disappears into a dark tunnel—they become afraid.

I want you to experience the same thing!

Not because I'm mean, but because it will be fun.

Really!

Taking that first step to have a family time might be a little scary at first—most adventures are—but don't worry. You won't be alone. I will be your guide. You won't get lost, and I'll make sure you don't eat too much cotton candy before going on the whirling teacups. In other words, you will be okay.

52 Creative Family Time Experiences is a journey of discovery, together. That means it will be fun. But like a thrilling amusement ride, it will require a little risk. It will be a journey—going to a place you have never been before. The good news is you won't even have to take the minivan! And you get to do it together.

> *Today's families don't seem to have much time for each other, and if we finally carve out time, we twiddle our thumbs, look at each other and ask, "So waddya wanna do?"*

52 Creative Family Time Experiences provides the structure and ideas for the meaningful and fun family time you want, helping you discover and experience God's timeless principles for strong families.

In just a few minutes each week you will discover treasures right in your own family. You will also be building lasting memories for you and your children.

I pray these experiences will launch a tradition of love, laughter, and learning together for your family, because *families really matter.*

A Few Tips To Get You Started

1. **Invest the time.** Ideally, set aside time each week. If you can, make it the same time during the week. If you are too busy, start with every other week. Children benefit from routine and will anticipate the time. If you choose a weekend Family Time, you may need to be flexible with other activities.

2. **Prepare.** Read the weekly session ahead of time and obtain the materials you will need. (A **Master Materials List** that summarizes what's needed for all the experiences is in the back of the book). You might even practice reading the Scripture text for maximum expression and impact.

3. **Protect** your Family Time by eliminating any distractions like texting, calls, TV, radio, video games, or the computer. You will need twenty minutes for the regular sessions and ninety minutes to two hours for the Movie Nights.

4. **Customize** for your kids. Refer to the *Adapting for preschool and teenagers* sections to adapt for your children.

5. **Honor** each other by having every family member present (if possible).

6. **Be flexible** and make it fun. Don't worry if your Family Time turns into a laugh-fest!

Each experience offers the following elements, sometimes in a different order:

- *Main Point*—for focus.
- *Materials Needed*—To help the parent prepare.
- *Warm Up*—To engage the children with a soft start.
- *Bible Readings*—To be read aloud. (Can also be used as a Memory Verse.)
- *Today's Slogan*—To repeat aloud as a fun, simple way to reinforce the aim.
- *Activity*—A fun, active experience using things you have around the house. Typically takes ten minutes. Some Movie Nights take longer.
- *Family Discussion*—A few questions to go deeper on the topic and to encourage transfer of learning and accountability. Including sections: "What does the Bible say?" and "What Should We Do?"
- *Adapting For*—Suggestions for younger children (Preschool and Primary) and teens.
- *Prayer*—The Family Time ends with a prayer that can be read aloud.

OPTION PLAYS

There are at least five ways to use *52 Creative Family Time Experiences*. You don't have to stick with one way—you can mix it up if you want. Like a skilled quarterback in football might call an option play—pass, hand off, or run it himself, as busy parents we need options.

1. **Weekly**—Pick a time that works best for your family. It doesn't have to be at night. It could be after pancakes on Saturday. You will need extra time for the Movie Nights. One family did the Movie Nights on Friday night and their other Family Time on Sunday

afternoons, right after lunch. Some families have found that **every other week** works best for their busy schedules.

2. **Family Weekend**—Get away for the weekend or go camping in the back yard! Design your own family retreat by choosing three or four Family Times and adding in some fun like swimming; biking; hiking; or going bowling at midnight.

3. **Vacation**—Dozens of our field-testing families reported that *52 Creative Family Time Experiences* worked great when they were on their summer vacation. Since they were traveling and away from their church, they were able to have spiritual times every day—in just twenty minutes a day. Try to adapt the family time to fit the unique setting of the place you are visiting.

4. **Daily**—Hundreds of our field-testing families participated everyday as part of a community or church campaign for thirty or forty days. This takes extra planning because the days come around so quickly, so try to prepare your materials in advance. Try gathering one week's worth of materials at a time. Some churches have purchased the book in bulk and used as a church-wide **Lent** or **Advent** faith at home campaign for forty days. Dozens of churches have adopted a *40 Days for The Family* emphasis.

5. **Holidays Only**—You may be looking for something new to do as a family for holidays and special occasions. Add some substance to Back to School, the New Year, and Independence Day by integrating the holiday session from *52 Creative Family Time Experiences.*

EXPERIENCE

• 1 •

Why Families?

MAIN POINT: God placed us in families to learn about Him, life, and love.

MATERIALS: Socks, bowls, and string.

WARM-UP

ASK: "Do parents ever get the day off? What would happen if parents took off for one day and did just what we wanted to—slept in, didn't go to work, played video games, or watched sports all day?"

BIBLE READING: Read aloud Deuteronomy 5:7–10:

You shall have no other gods before me. You shall not make for yourself a carved image, or any likeness of anything that is in heaven above, or that is on the earth beneath, or that is in the water under the earth. You shall not bow down to them or serve them; for I the LORD your God am a jealous God, visiting the iniquity of the fathers on the children to the third and fourth generation of those who hate me, but showing steadfast love to thousands of those who love me and keep my commandments. (ESV)

FAMILY DISCUSSION

God placed us in families to learn about Him, life, and love.

1. ASK: "Why does God warn, 'No other gods, only me?'" (God deserves first place in our lives.)

2. God expects parents to tell their kids about the true God.
   ASK: "How do parents do that?"(By *telling* their kids
   about the real God in contrast to the fake gods that hu-
   mans make. Parents also *show* what God is like by being
   kind and obedient and setting an example themselves of
   what they are trying to teach their kids.)

ACTIVITY: BOWLS OF MERCY SOCK TOSS

Get ten clean pairs of socks and roll each up in a ball. Get ten
bowls of various sizes. Tape a number (1–10) on each bowl. Make
a line with string at least three feet away from the bowls. One at
a time, each family member stands behind the line and tosses
ten sock balls, trying to land one in each bowl. Keep score.

TODAY'S SLOGAN: "God comes first in my life." (Repeat
several times, together)

ADAPTING FOR . . .

YOUNGER CHILDREN: For the Family Discussion,
ASK: "We learn about love and God in our family. When do
you feel loved?" After the Activity; skip the Wrap Up, but **SAY:**
"Families that love each other try to help each other be good by
putting God first."

TEENS: Move the string line back for teens to six feet away
from the bowls. During the Debrief time, **ASK:** "What would
happen in a family that didn't have any rules? What would it be
like if lying, stealing, and being mean was okay?"

WRAP UP

ASK: "What was it like trying to land a sock in each bowl?"

1. **SAY:** "The ten bowls represent God's Ten Commandments. Today's Scripture is one of God's Ten Commandments. The first few verses talk about putting God first in our lives. This isn't easy because we'd rather put ourselves first. Trying to land a sock in each bowl is hard to do too. But there is a reward…"

2. **ASK:** "What promise does God make to those who love Him and keep His commandments?" (That He will be lovingly loyal to them.)

WHAT SHOULD WE DO?

What are some ways we "put God first in our lives"? (By thinking of Him first; by knowing what He says and obeying Him; and by wanting to know Him as much as wanting to get something.)

PRAYER

Dear Heavenly Father, You are awesome, powerful and You alone deserve first place in our lives. Help us to remember today that You come first. In Jesus' name, Amen.

EXPERIENCE

• 2 •

We Need Reminders

MAIN POINT: Families remind each other of the good things about each other and about God.

MATERIALS: A ball of yarn.

WARM UP

Have everyone describe a time when they forgot something. (Hear two or three examples). **SAY:** "It is easy to forget. As families, we can help each other remember important things."

BIBLE READING: Read aloud Deuteronomy 6:6–9:

And these words that I command you today shall be on your heart. You shall teach them diligently to your children, and shall talk of them when you sit in your house, and when you walk by the way, and when you lie down, and when you rise. You shall bind them as a sign on your hand, and they shall be as frontlets between your eyes. You shall write them on the doorposts of your house and on your gates. (ESV)

FAMILY DISCUSSION

WHAT DOES THE BIBLE SAY?

ASK: "Why does God want us to remember His commandments?" (So we will obey them.)

WHAT SHOULD WE DO?

ASK: "What are the different ways parents help their kids learn and remember God's commandments?" (Memorize; talk as you sit or walk—in the morning; at bedtime; attach them to your head and hands and around the house.)

ACTIVITY: SPIDER WEB

Holding a ball of yarn; have everyone stand in a circle, spaced about four feet from each other. (This works best if there are four or more people.) Hold the end of the yarn and **SAY:** "Whoever catches the ball has to say two things—something good that he likes about the person who threw the ball and something good about God."

Everyone hangs on to the yarn with one hand and tosses with the other. Soon you will have a spider web of affirmation and gratefulness.

After several tosses, **SAY:** "You can also say what you are thankful for." Continue until you have a beautiful spider web pattern. **ASK:** "What does this web do to us?" (Holds us together; makes us a team.)

TODAY'S SLOGAN: "Good things are worth remembering." (Repeat several times)

ADAPTING FOR . . .

YOUNGER CHILDREN: Simplify the activity with the instruction: **SAY:** "Whoever catches the ball has to say one thing nice about the person they are throwing it to."

TEENS: Extend the Discussion and **ASK:** "Which of these faith-building exercises works best with you? Memorizing; sitting and talking about them; thinking about them on walks; in the morning; at meals or at bedtime?" **ASK:** "What happens if somebody drops his yarn?" (It ruins the web and makes us weak.)

NOTE: After a few sessions of you leading the family time, ask your teens to handle part or all of one of the sessions. We have found that if teens are involved in some way, that they tend to get more out of Family Times because they "aren't treated like a kid."

PRAYER

Dear Heavenly Father, help us to remember the important things You have done, and who You are. Help us to also remember each other and be thankful for each other; knowing that together, we are strong. In Christ's name, Amen.

EXPERIENCE
•3•   Family Traditions

MAIN POINT: Our family strength and unity comes from God.

MATERIALS: Broomstick, twine, tape, and paper

WARM UP

1. **ASK:** "What are some different kinds of tests?" (Tests at school; skills tests; tryouts to make the athletic team; driver's test; tests to get into some schools, etc.)
2. **ASK:** "What do tests and tryouts show?" (If we know something or can do something.)

BIBLE READING: Read aloud Deuteronomy 8:2, 11–16:

And you shall remember the whole way that the LORD your God has led you these forty years in the wilderness, that he might humble you, testing you to know what was in your heart, whether you would keep his commandments or not. Take care lest you forget the LORD your God by not keeping his commandments and his rules and his statutes, which I command you today, lest, when you have eaten and are full and have built good houses and live in them, and when your herds and flocks multiply and your silver and gold is multiplied and all that you have is multiplied, then your heart be lifted up, and you forget the LORD your God, who brought you out of the land of Egypt, out of the house of slavery, who led you through the great and terrifying wilderness, with its fiery serpents and scorpions and thirsty ground where there was no water, who brought you water out of the flinty rock, who fed you in the wilderness with manna that your fathers did not know, that he might humble you and test you, to do you good in the end. (ESV)

FAMILY DISCUSSION

WHAT DOES THE BIBLE SAY?

ASK: "Why does God test us?" (To help us get stronger; To learn to depend on Him.)

WHAT SHOULD WE DO?

ASK: "Why would it be easy to forget God if life was going really well? (We feel we don't need Him and look to our stuff and money for security.)

ACTIVITY: LET'S PULL TOGETHER

(This works best on carpet). Gather a three- to four foot-piece of dowel, broomstick, yardstick, or mop handle; twine; a piece of paper; marker and tape. On the paper, write the slogan in big letters and tape to the side of the stick, about two inches from one end. Cut the twine into six-foot pieces—one for each family member. **SAY:** "The stick, twine, and slogan represent our family unity. We need to pull together if we are going to stand together in difficult times (as the Hebrews did in the wilderness)." Have each person tie her string a little above the halfway point of the stick. Lay the stick down on the floor and gather the family in a circle around it. Each person holds the end of his or her string. **ASK** one child, "Try to raise the stick and stand it up on end by pulling on your string." (It won't work.) Ask two children to try to raise the stick by pulling. (It might work.) Then **SAY:** "Let's all pull together." The object of the activity is to stand the stick up straight with each person maintaining

tension on the stick with their string. The stick should stand up.
SAY: "With everyone doing his or her part, we are able to stand tall against the challenges. **ASK:** "What happens if one person isn't connected?" (Let go of your string. The stick will drop or fall.) **SAY:** "Everybody is needed in this family. We are strong when we pull together."

TODAY'S SLOGAN: "We are strong when we pull together."

ADAPTING FOR . . .

YOUNGER CHILDREN: Skip Warm Up question 2. For the Activity, sit on the floor in a circle with your feet surrounding the stick. Make the stick shorter, two to three feet in length. If they can't pull the stick up; try standing it up with your hand and holding it up with the strings. Pre-school children often don't have the coordination for precise pulling and balance, so help them succeed at making the stick stand up straight.

TEENS: After the activity, **ASK:** "Describe a time when we need to pull together as a family." (Example: "When I am learning to drive, you shouldn't make fun of me.")

PRAYER

Dear Heavenly Father, Thank You that we have each other. Help us to learn all we can from the tests of life. Help us to support each other so we can be strong and stand straight in the middle of life's tests. In Jesus' name, Amen.

•4•

Sand Castles or Monuments?

MAIN POINT: A child's curiosity provides opportunities to teach spiritual truths.

MATERIALS: Twelve smooth river stones (3-4 inches each) and permanent markers.

WARM UP

ASK: "Remember when we visited the ocean and the water washed over our sand castle? What happens to a sand castle if we build it too close to the water?" (The tide comes up and the waves knock it down.) "How long would it last if we built it far away from the waves?" (A few days.) "What would be a better building material than sand?" (Rocks, bricks, wood, etc., because they last.)

BIBLE READING: Read aloud Joshua 4:4–7:

Then Joshua called the twelve men whom he had appointed from the children of Israel, one man from every tribe; and Joshua said to them: "Cross over before the ark of the LORD your God into the midst of the Jordan, and each one of you take up a stone on his shoulder, according to the number of the tribes of the children of Israel, that this may be a sign among you when your children ask in time to come, saying, 'What do these stones mean to you?' Then you shall answer them that the waters of the Jordan were cut off before the ark of the covenant of the LORD; when it crossed over the Jordan, the waters of the Jordan were cut off. And these stones shall be for a memorial to the children of Israel forever." (NKJV)

FAMILY DISCUSSION

WHAT DOES THE BIBLE SAY?

1. **ASK:** "Why do you think God told them to use stones?" (Because they last longer than sand and they are everywhere; don't have to buy them.)
2. **ASK:** "What were the stones for?" (To remind us that the Jordan River stopped flowing and the Ark of the Lord's covenant went across the dry riverbed.)

WHAT SHOULD WE DO?

ASK: "What are some ways we can use stones or rocks to help us remember the miracles God did for His people?" (Write on rocks and leave them around the house or garden.)

ACTIVITY: THE ROCKS CRY OUT

Purchase twelve smooth river stones (about 3 to 4 inches each) from your home improvement center or gardening supply. Divide the rocks evenly among the family members. **ASK:** "What are some ways God has been faithful to us?" One at a time, have each person explain how he or she has seen God at work. Then, using permanent markers write on the stones how God has been faithful to your family. After you are finished, display your rocks inside or in the garden as a memorial and tribute to God's work in your family.

TODAY'S SLOGAN: "A faith that rocks is one that remembers."

ADAPTING FOR . . .

YOUNGER CHILDREN: Instead of describing in words, younger kids can draw pictures of what they are thankful for on the rocks. Don't use permanent markers. Use washable markers.

TEENS: ASK: "How will you explain the rock garden to your friends when they come over?" and "What should we name our rock garden?" Ask them if they would like to make a sign with the name.

PRAYER

Thank You God that You remember us. You never forget about us. We are precious in Your sight. Help us to remember all You have done for us. In the name of Your Son, Jesus, Amen.

EXPERIENCE

•5•　　Love Doesn't Quit

MAIN POINT: Love never gives up.

MATERIALS: Popcorn and the movie *Finding Nemo*.

WARM UP

Pop some popcorn and get cozy around the TV. **SAY:** "Can you think of three stories that show that love never gives up?" (Any story will do, but you could also mention that God's story is a love story too!)

BIBLE READING: Read aloud 1 Corinthians 13:4–7:

> *Love is patient and kind. Love is not jealous or boastful or proud or rude. It does not demand its own way. It is not irritable, and it keeps no record of being wronged. It does not rejoice about injustice but rejoices whenever the truth wins out.* **Love never gives up,** *never loses faith, is always hopeful, and endures through every circumstance. [Emphasis added] (NLT)*

ACTIVITY: FINDING NEMO

Introduce the movie and **SAY:** "Tonight we are going to watch a movie about the love between a father and a son. The kind of love that withstands all kinds of problems."

TIME SAVER: If you don't have time to watch the entire movie, watch as much as you can and then skip to the "Reunion" scene near the end (Scene 29 on DVD). Adjust the Family Discussion accordingly.

FAMILY DISCUSSION

ASK:

1. "What part of the movie did you like?"
2. "What do you think Nemo learned about his father's love for him?"
3. "What did Nemo's dad do to show his love for his son?" (Crossed the ocean to search for his son.)
4. "Nemo's dad (Marlin) was really protective of his son. What are some ways human parents protect their children?"

TODAY'S SLOGAN: "Love never gives up."

ADAPTING FOR . . .

YOUNGER CHILDREN: Skip the Warm Up question and begin with the Scripture, followed by your introduction of the movie. You may choose to show only part of the movie to accommodate the attention span of preschool age children. Or you may prefer to show the movie in multiple settings. After the movie, skip Discussion question 2 & 4.

TEENS: After the movie, **ASK:** "Describe a time when parents AND teens need to hang in there and not give up."

PRAYER

Dear Heavenly Father, thank You for Your love that never gives up on us. Even with problems and bad things, Your love never gives up. You sent Jesus to this planet so we could be with You. Thank You that You go great distances to show Your love for us. In Jesus' name, Amen.

EXPERIENCE
•6•

Family Is Still a Good Idea

MAIN POINT: The family is God's idea.

MATERIALS: Park with playground equipment or indoor mall if the weather is too severe; toy blocks or dominoes.

WARM UP

ASK: "How would life be different if there were no families?" (Entertain a few responses, even some wild ones.)

BIBLE READING: Read aloud Deuteronomy 7:9:

Know therefore that the LORD your God is God, the faithful God who keeps covenant and steadfast love with those who love him and keep his commandments, to a thousand generations. (ESV)

FAMILY DISCUSSION

WHAT DOES THE BIBLE SAY?

1. **SAY:** "God designed the family so that parents can help their children know the truth about Him and His world. It's the parents' job to help their children know and love God." (Line up several blocks in a row.)
2. **ASK:** "Do you know what a generation is?" (Parents are one generation, their kids are the next generation, and

when you become a parent your kids will be the third generation.) Indicate three generations with three blocks. You can set them up like dominoes, so they will knock each other over as you touch the one on the end.

WHAT SHOULD WE DO?

1. **ASK:** "How can God pass on His love to a thousand generations?" (One parent and one child at a time.)
2. **SAY:** "Today we will see how parents can pass on something good to their children and they can pass it on to their kids. It's a chain of good things.

ACTIVITY: PLAYGROUND PARABLE

Go to a neighborhood park or playground that has swings or climbing apparatus. Spend fifteen minutes climbing, hanging, swinging, and sliding. Try playing *Follow the Leader* and have a child be the leader—everyone has to copy what he does—including the parents! Try to emphasize that in families we *Follow the Leader* and we pass on good things to the younger ones.

TODAY'S SLOGAN: "Family is a good idea because it's God's idea."

ADAPTING FOR . . .

YOUNGER CHILDREN: Choose a park with equipment designed for pre-schoolers. If weather doesn't permit outdoor activity, go to a mall that has indoor playground equipment.

TEENS: Go to the park at night so there's less of a chance that your teen's friends will see him! Afterward, reward them with an ice cream cone. If weather doesn't permit, then consider doing another indoor activity where you can "follow" each other; like ice-skating, roller-skating, bowling, or scaling an indoor climbing wall.

PRAYER

Dear Father God, We praise You for making our family. We praise You for including us in Your family. Thank You for making us part of the chain of blessing for a thousand generations. We will be careful to pass on Your love. In Jesus' name, Amen.

EXPERIENCE

•7•

The Worry-Hurry Connection

MAIN POINT: We need to stop ourselves from always being in a hurry.

MATERIALS: Red construction paper, scissors, markers, and tape. Some kids are very slow paper cutters, up to second or third grade, so it might be good to plan on cutting out the octagons beforehand, providing stencils, or trace them on paper.

WARM UP

SAY: "Today we are going to slow down, sit in one place and have time for each other, but it's going to be kind of weird. We are going to have a staring contest!" Sit in a circle on the floor. Look each person in the eye and stare. Try not to blink. If you blink, you are eliminated from the circle.

BIBLE READING: Read aloud Philippians 4:6-7:

Don't worry about anything; instead, pray about everything. Tell God what you need, and thank him for all he has done. Then you will experience God's peace, which exceeds anything we can understand. His peace will guard your hearts and minds as you live in Christ Jesus. (NLT)

FAMILY DISCUSSION

SAY: "In this Family Time we start looking at reasons why we are in such a hurry. Today's reason is that *our culture likes a fast pace.* Nobody likes to go slow. It seems like we are becoming more hurried.

WHAT DOES THE BIBLE SAY?

ASK: "Instead of worrying, what are we supposed to do?" (Pray.)

WHAT SHOULD WE DO?

1. **ASK:** "Do you think our family is in a hurry very often? When does that happen?"
2. **ASK:** "How does our modern world make it possible for us to do things fast? "What are some of the things we do that are fast?" (Fast food; drive-thrus; microwave dinners; computers; over-night deliveries; downloading music; email; etc.)
3. **ASK:** "Is it always good to be in a hurry? When is it better to slow down?"

ACTIVITY: STOP SIGNS

Using construction paper, scissors, and markers; make an octagon to be used for a stop sign. Discuss the phrases from the Scripture that might help us stop the hurry, and write them on your signs: "STOP," "Don't Worry!" or "Pray!" etc. Post these around the house as reminders to focus on God's peace and not always rushing.

TODAY'S SLOGAN: "God's peace helps us not need to hurry."

ADAPTING FOR . . .

YOUNGER CHILDREN: Early writers might enjoy having their signs pre-made with the words very lightly written or done in dots for them to trace. Shorten the discussion by asking, "When do you like to go fast?" and "When do you like to go slow or stop?" For the activity, pre-cut the Stop signs.

TEENS: ASK: "Why is it important for you to obey traffic signs, as you learn to drive?" and "What might happen, if all teen drivers ignored traffic signs and signals?" Ask them to post the sign in their room as a reminder to ask God for peace when they feel stressed or rushed.

PRAYER

Help us God to not be in such a hurry that we don't take time for each other. Help us to take time to talk with You about everything, so we can have Your peace in our hearts and minds. In Jesus' name, Amen.

EXPERIENCE
·8·

Escape from Hurry at Work and School

MAIN POINT: Speed doesn't always work as well at home.

MATERIALS: Baby food, spoon, juice, sipper cup, and bib.

WARM UP

What was your least favorite baby food? What was your favorite? (If the child has difficult remembering, mom could probably recall.)

BIBLE READING: Read aloud 1 Thessalonians 2:7b-8:

> *We were like a mother feeding and caring for her own children. We loved you so much that we shared with you not only God's Good News but our own lives, too. (NLT)*

FAMILY DISCUSSION

1. **ASK:** "Have you noticed that you can't hurry babies when they are eating?" (Some kids may not have noticed this.) **SAY:** "One thing I learned when you were babies is that you can't be hurried. You liked to take your time with the bottle and enjoy each swallow. As you got older, you liked to *experience* your food; not necessarily eat it! It might be in your hair, on the walls, on the floor, and a little bit might actually get in your mouth!" **ASK:** "Why do you think you can't rush babies?"

2. **ASK:** "Do you ever feel rushed to finish your work at school?"

WHAT DOES THE BIBLE SAY?

ASK: "Why is it important to be gentle when feeding and caring for babies?" (We shouldn't always rush; instead, we should take time to care for one another and give one another what we need.)

WHAT SHOULD WE DO?

ASK: "Are there some things we do that are hurried or rushed? What are some things that might be better if we slowed down?" (Example: family meals)

ACTIVITY: BIG BABY

Do a role reversal and have your kids feed *you* baby food and juice from a sipper cup. Make sure you wear a bib. Have them feed you as fast as they can spoon it up. After a jar of baby food, debrief with them about the experience. **ASK:** "Was it fun? Weird? Aren't you glad we don't do that every day?" etc.

TODAY'S SLOGAN: "Doing things faster isn't always better."

ADAPTING FOR . . .

YOUNGER CHILDREN: Skip questions 3 & 4 in the Discussion. If your child is at least four years old, she should be able to do this activity. If she is younger, have one parent feed the other. If there is only one parent, feed yourself! Then discuss what she thought about watching you.

TEENS: They are going to love this activity as is! Wear old clothes.

PRAYER

Dear Father God, help us to not always be in a hurry. Give us patience and understanding at home, school, and work. Help us to make time for each other, because we love each other. In Jesus' name, Amen.

EXPERIENCE
•9•

It Takes Time to Grow Up

MAIN POINT: There is nothing *instant* about maturity.

MATERIALS: Pencil, butcher paper (or heavy duty plain wrapping paper) scissors, and markers.

WARM UP

With a pencil, mark everyone's height on a door jam. **ASK:** "Can you get taller by wishing you were taller?" (No) **SAY:** "Growth takes time. When we get older, it's called becoming 'mature'. We grow physically—get taller and bigger—but what are some other ways to grow." (Emotionally, mentally, etc.)

BIBLE READING: Read aloud Ephesians 4:11-13:

> *God handed out gifts above and below, filled heaven with his gifts, filled earth with his gifts. He handed out gifts of apostle, prophet, evangelist, and pastor-teacher to train Christians in skilled servant work, working within Christ's body, the church, until we're all moving rhythmically and easily with each other, efficient and graceful in response to God's Son, fully mature adults, fully developed within and without, fully alive in Christ. No prolonged infancies among us, please. We'll not tolerate babes in the woods, small children who are an easy mark for imposters.* **God wants us to grow up,** *to know the whole truth and tell it in love—like Christ in everything.* (MSG) [emphasis added]

Check to make sure your child understands the more difficult words in this Scripture.

FAMILY DISCUSSION

WHAT DOES THE BIBLE SAY?

1. **ASK:** "What does God give us to help us grow up?" (Each other to help each other; everyone has a position to play on God's team.)
2. **ASK:** "What are some things that help us grow physically?" (Good food, sleep, exercise, clean water.) "Can we see the growth right away? If I eat my vegetables tonight will I be bigger and stronger in the morning?" (No)

WHAT SHOULD WE DO?

ASK: "What do we need to grow with each other as a family?" (Time together, being kind to each other, safe home, protect each other. These take time and added together over the years make a healthy home. It takes time to grow a family).

ACTIVITY: GOOD GIANT

Using a pencil and butcher or wrapping paper, trace the tallest person in your family, by having them lie on the paper. Then make him or her taller by adding a few inches to the neck and legs. Have each family member think of one thing that will help grow the giant physically and draw that on or near him (vegetables, milk, etc.). Also have each family member think of one thing that will help grow in maturity and character (by getting along with others: being kind, protecting others from harm, saying nice things, not running in the house, etc.). Display the giant where you will see him as a reminder that it's important to grow up.

TODAY'S SLOGAN: "Growing up isn't baby stuff."

ADAPTING FOR . . .

YOUNGER CHILDREN: During the Discussion, skip question 3. For the Activity, simplify the discussion and ASK: "What do kids need to grow big?" (Milk, vegetables, meat, sleep, exercise ...)

TEENS: For older teens, you may want to skip the Activity and extend the discussion, and ASK: "The Scripture talks about growing up with truth and love. Why are truth and love essential for growing up?" As an alternative activity, you could make a poster of the things we need to grow up. Draw a stick figure with dialogue bubbles (like comics) of several essentials for growing up.

PRAYER

God, help us to grow up and not be babies. Help us to be mature and know the truth and tell it in love. In Jesus' name, Amen.

EXPERIENCE

•10•

Learning Contentment

MAIN POINT: Contentment makes me flexible.

MATERIALS: Dictionary, a can of peaches, spoons, bowls, and can opener.

WARM UP

ASK: "What is something you would like right now as a gift? (A toy, doll, motorcycle, clothes, etc.) "Where did you learn about this cool thing?" (Probably on TV or from friends.)

BIBLE READING: Read aloud Philippians 4:11–12:

> Not that I am speaking of being in need, for I have learned in whatever situation I am to be content. I know how to be brought low, and I know how to abound. In any and every circumstance, I have learned the secret of facing plenty and hunger, abundance and need. (ESV)

FAMILY DISCUSSION

SAY: "There's nothing wrong with wanting cool things; like toys, bikes and clothes; but when we want things *too* much, it can lead to problems."

WHAT DOES THE BIBLE SAY?

SAY: "Contentment means to learn how to get along happily with little or much. It's the 'being full' feeling, instead of feeling empty." **ASK**: "Can you think of a time when you felt this way?"

WHAT SHOULD WE DO?

Look up *contentment* in the dictionary and discuss it. **ASK**: "How does contentment help us at home?" (We learn to be happy with what we have and thankful for it.)

ACTIVITY: CONTENTED PEACHES

Get a can of peaches, can opener, bowls, and spoons. Pass around the can and call attention to the "contents." It might say "24 ounces of peaches in their juice." Food products are required to have the content description on them. **ASK**: "What would you think if we opened this can of peaches and there were snails inside?" Open the can. **ASK**: "How would you feel if the can was half empty? The contents are full." Show that the can is full. We are content when we are full. When we focus on what we don't have, we are not content, but whiny and wanting." Spoon up the peaches into bowls and enjoy!

TODAY'S SLOGAN: "Happy with little or happy with much, makes me happy."

ADAPTING FOR . . .

YOUNGER CHILDREN: Skip the Discussion and **ASK**: "Sometimes we have to stop wanting and be happy with what we have. What do you have that makes you happy?"

TEENS: After the Activity, **ASK**: "What can we do to remind ourselves to be content and not whining about what we don't have?" (Examples: display the empty peach can; display a glass of milk half-full, etc.)

PRAYER

Dear Heavenly Father, help us to be satisfied with what we have, and not be running after the latest thing we think we must have. In Jesus' name, Amen.

EXPERIENCE

• 11 •

The Power of Not Giving Up

MAIN POINT: God gives us strength to not give up.

MATERIALS: *UP* animated movie by Disney Pixar and popcorn.

WARM UP

Pop some popcorn and gather around the TV. **ASK:** "What are some things that we get better at if we keep trying?" (Building blocks, learning to ride a bike, coloring, toilet training, sports, etc.) **ASK:** "What does it take to get better at something?" (Practice, doing it over and over, and willingness to learn.)

BIBLE READING: Read aloud Philippians 4:13:

For I can do everything through Christ, who gives me strength. (NLT)

WHAT DOES THE BIBLE SAY?
ASK: "What can we do with Christ's help?" (Everything)

ACTIVITY

MOVIE: *UP*—enjoy the movie together.

FAMILY DISCUSSION

1. **SAY:** "Today's session is about not giving up. We saw scenes of not giving up in the movie, like Russell, the Wilderness Explorer knocking on Carl Fredericksen's door, and asking

him, "Are you in need of help?" Even though the door kept closing on him, Russell kept trying. **ASK:** "What does that tell us about not giving up?"

2. **ASK:** "What were some other scenes from the movie about not giving up?" (Carl staying with Ellie through her illness. Carl pursuing his dream of going to South America, etc.)

3. **ASK:** "What are some things you have to do, that are hard and make you feel like giving up?" (Homework, cleaning my room, yard work.)

TODAY'S SLOGAN: "God's strength helps me not give up."

ADAPTING FOR . . .

YOUNGER CHILDREN: Watch the movie until after the scene where Russell is knocking on Carl's door and **ASK:** "Why was it good that Russell kept trying?" **ASK:** "What are some things that are hard to do, but you can do them now because you kept trying?" (Learned to tie my shoes; dress myself; stack blocks; clean up my toys . . .)

TEENS: This time, the teens get to ask the questions. **ASK** your mom or dad, "Describe a time when you were persistent and hung in there, against the odds?" **ASK:** "What made the difference? Why didn't you give up?" Reflecting on the montage of Carl and Ellie's lives over time; **ASK:** "Like Carl and Ellie went through all kinds of seasons, what kinds of seasons have you been through?"

PRAYER

(If you want, you can mention some of the needs that were discussed from discussion question #3.) Dear Heavenly Father, sometimes we feel like giving up. We feel like quitting. Give us Your strength to hang in there. (Example: Give *Jennifer* the strength to study for her test . . .)

·12·

WWF—World Wrestling Families

MAIN POINT: Sometimes our selfishness causes fights.

MATERIALS: Paper and pen.

WARM UP

For the Parent(s) to answer: "What did you do as a child to scheme to get your way?" (If you cannot recall anything, or if your example is not appropriate, create or find such a story.)

BIBLE READING: Read aloud James 4:1-3:

What causes quarrels and what causes fights among you? Is it not this, that your passions are at war within you? You desire and do not have, so you murder. You covet and cannot obtain, so you fight and quarrel. You do not have, because you do not ask. You ask and do not receive, because you ask wrongly, to spend it on your passions. (ESV)

FAMILY DISCUSSION

ASK: "Besides air, water, and sun, what would be hard to live without?" (List the items on a large sheet of paper.) ASK: "What do you need to get through the day?"

WHAT DOES THE BIBLE SAY? (Re-read the Bible reading)

ASK: "Sometimes what we want gets in the way of getting along with others. What are some of the problems listed in the Scripture?" (Fighting, evil desires, scheming, killing, jealousy.)

WHAT SHOULD WE DO?

ASK: "What makes life comfortable for you?" (Expand the list until you have at least a dozen comfort-producing things: iPod, cell phone, microwave, computer, TV, video games, etc.)

ACTIVITY: FAMILY SURVIVOR

SAY: "Imagine that our plane crashed in the warm waters of the South Pacific. Our family is the only survivors. We are in a life raft with all of this stuff (point to the list just written) and it's too heavy. If we are going to make it to the island a mile away, we have to get rid of the extra baggage. What would you get rid of first? And you can't say, 'My little brother.'"

Each person takes turns crossing off one item and explains why they chose that one. Accept their decision. Don't argue about it. Keep taking turns until there is only one item left. Discuss why the final item is important to your family.

TODAY'S SLOGAN: "The most important things in life aren't things."

ADAPTING FOR . . .

YOUNGER CHILDREN: Instead of the Survivor story (too scary for little ones). **ASK:** "Let's say you are going to visit grandma or a friend for the night. What would you put in your backpack (or overnight bag)?" "What would you *need* to take?"

TEENS: ASK: "What are some ways life is like a life raft—forcing us to make hard choices?" (We don't have time or money to do all that we want. Some choices compete against each other.)

PRAYER

Father God, help us to remember that people are more important than things. Teach us to not be selfish. In Jesus' name, Amen.

Why We Rush

> **MAIN POINT:** We rush for many reasons; most of them are not healthy.
>
> **MATERIALS:** Car to drive to a health club, sporting goods store, or pet store.

WARM UP

Gather the family in one room. Have them wait for you while you go into the other room and put on lots of heavy gear (helmet, hiking boots, trench coat, backpack, goggles, etc.) then come out and **SAY:** "I am ready to run a race! Who wants to race me?" "Do I look ready to run?" "Why not?" Take off each item as you offer a lame reason for wearing it. "I was going to wear the goggles so no bugs would get into my eyes while I ran." At the end, **ASK:** "How do you prepare to run?" (By wearing nothing that hinders you or slows you down.)

BIBLE READING: Read aloud 1 Corinthians 9:24:

> *Do you know that in a race all the runners run, but only one receives the prize? So run that you may obtain it. (ESV)*

FAMILY DISCUSSION

WHAT DOES THE BIBLE SAY?

ASK: "Who runs the race?" (Everyone) "How many win?" (only one) "What's the key to winning?" (Be faster than everyone else.)

SAY: "Here are 5 *Reasons Why We Rush*: these seem like good ideas, but like the stuff I was wearing for my race, they actually aren't helpful."

1. We like the latest things like toys, music, and fashion.
2. We want to do lots of things in a short amount of time. We hate wasting time.
3. We expect fast service and fast technology (computers, etc.).
4. We, as a family, want to have and do lots of things but there isn't time to get them all without hurrying.
5. We are running from something. (We don't want to face the past; we are afraid to slow down and feel; or we are nervous about the future.)

ASK: "Which of these do you see as reasons why we (as a family) rush?"

ACTIVITY: TOUR TREADMILLS

It's time to get out of the house for just a few minutes. Take a quick tour of your health club or request to walk through one in your neighborhood. All you want to look at are the treadmills. Another place you can see them are at sporting goods stores. **ASK** your kids, "Can you get anywhere running on one of these?" Another option is to go to a pet store and watch the hamsters spinning around on their wheels. "You can't run to win if you are running in circles."

TODAY'S SLOGAN: "Run to win."

ADAPTING FOR . . .

YOUNGER CHILDREN: Explain the reasons for rushing in terms they'd understand and provide examples. "Would you rather be in the front of the line or the back of the line to go down the slide at the park?" Instead of driving somewhere, have your kids run in place and pump their legs faster and faster.

TEENS: Extend the Discussion and **ASK:** "Do you think adults are more hurried than teens? Why?" After the **Activity**, **ASK:** "What are some ways we, as family members, look like hamsters on the wheel or runners on the treadmill, frantically running in place but not getting anywhere?" "What can we do about it?"

PRAYER

God help us not to run foolishly just because everyone else is, but to discover the right speed for our family. In Jesus' name, Amen.

EXPERIENCE ·14·

Sold Out

MAIN POINT: Our priorities reveal what is in our heart.

MATERIALS: Fake Check (you can draw it), butcher paper, pencils, rulers, crayons, and markers.

WARM UP

SAY: "We just won the magazine sweepstakes! Some guy dropped off a check at our front door for $50,000!" (Show fake check.) "What should we do with the money?" (Take turns responding. If somebody doesn't suggest it, bring up the idea of fixing up the house.)

BIBLE READING: Read aloud Deuteronomy 6:5:

You shall love the LORD your God with all your heart and with all your soul and with all your might. (ESV)

FAMILY DISCUSSION

1. **ASK:** "If the center of the home is where we hang out the most, what is the center of our home?"
2. **ASK:** "What is your favorite place in your house? Why?"

WHAT DOES THE BIBLE SAY?

ASK: "How should we love the Lord?" (With all that we are. All of us.)

ASK: "If we love God completely, it will show in how we act. What can we expect to see in the life of someone who loves God with all that he/she is?" (Likes to sing praises, learn about God, read the Bible, help people in need, etc.)

ACTIVITY: HOME MAKEOVER

Get out butcher paper or white shelf paper, pencils, rulers, and crayons or markers, and cut a two-foot piece of butcher paper for each person. **SAY:** "You are going to design your dream house. It can be anything you want it to be, but you only have four minutes to draw it. Go." When time is up, **SAY:** "You now have thirty seconds to describe your dream house." Take turns.

Then **SAY:** "Those were great, but they were just *houses*. A pretty house is not a home. What makes a *home*?" (List those ideas on paper, for example, love, patience, kindness, respect, etc.) **ASK:** "How can we illustrate these?" You might want to have these drawn on sticky notes or other small papers to stick/tape onto your house drawing. Draw a rough blueprint of your house, take the ideas for illustrating the qualities, and place them in various rooms. (Example: Sharing the bathroom requires patience.)

TODAY'S SLOGAN: "Loving God demands all of us."

ADAPTING FOR . . .

YOUNGER CHILDREN: Help them understand the abstract concepts of heart, soul, and strength. For instance, with "heart," we aren't talking about the muscle in our chest that pumps blood. We are thinking of that part of us that wishes and feels. "Soul" is that part of us that loves and worships God, and "strength" is in our bodies and what we can do with them, how we can serve others.

TEENS: ASK: "What would a teen look like—behavior-wise and in his choices, who loved God with ALL of his heart, soul, and strength?"

PRAYER

Help us to love You Lord with all of our heart, soul, and strength, in every room of our house and in every area of our lives. In Jesus' name, Amen.

Heart Guard

MAIN POINT: We need to protect our heart because it influences our choices.

MATERIALS: Clear glass jar, walnut-sized rocks, marbles, sand, bowls, and masking tape.

WARM UP

ASK: "What would you do with an extra three hours each day? Let's say we can magically make each day into a 27-hour day for just our family? What would you do with the extra time?"

BIBLE READING: Read aloud Proverbs 4:23:

Keep vigilant watch over your heart; that's where life starts. (MSG)

ACTIVITY: TIME JAR

Gather a clear glass jar (mayonnaise or canning jar), some rocks (about the size of a walnut, or use walnuts), marbles, and sand (or rice). With masking tape or a sticker, label the jar with "24 Hours." Before Family Time, fill the jar to the top with the rocks; add the marbles; then pour in the sand. Then empty the jar and separate the rocks, marbles, and sand into three bowls.

Gather your children and **SAY:** "This is a Time Jar. It represents all of the time we have in one day. The rocks are for the *hard* things we have to do—chores, homework, go to work, practice the clarinet, etc. The marbles stand for the regular stuff that isn't hard, but we just do in the day—like brush our teeth, eat our vegetables, and get to bed on time. The sand stands for all of the fun stuff we do in a day. The easy things like playing, watching TV, video games, and eating sweets. Working together we will fill up our Time Jar with what we'd want to do." (Take turns filling the jar, describing each activity as you go.)

Then **SAY:** "We have to watch what we fill our day with, or we won't fit it all in. If we begin taking care of the harder things (put the rocks in), we will have time for the medium things (put the marbles in), and the fun stuff (put the sand in)." But if we start with only the easy and fun stuff, we can't fit it all in.

FAMILY DISCUSSION

1. **ASK:** "What would happen if we filled up our time with nothing but fun stuff?"
2. **ASK:** "Why does it work one way, but not the other? Why can't we do the fun stuff first, and then work in the harder?" (Because it won't fit.)

WHAT DOES THE BIBLE SAY?

ASK: "*Vigilant* means 'careful.' How do we have to be careful about the part of us that wishes and feels?"

WHAT SHOULD WE DO?

ASK: "Protecting our heart means being careful with what we see and do. What are some things that might be around us, but not healthy for our hearts?"

TODAY'S SLOGAN: "Watch your heart and you'll have a good start."

ADAPTING FOR . . .

YOUNGER CHILDREN: The concept of the "heart" is too abstract for pre-school children. Like in the previous session, remind them here we are not talking about the organ that pumps blood, but we are talking about the part of them that wishes and dreams. For a pre-school child, the "heart" is the imagination; it is his "wisher."

TEENS: ASK: "Where do we see an emphasis on the heart?" (Popular music and culture.) **ASK:** "Why are teens so interested in issues of the heart?" (They are hoping for romance and are dreaming of the future.)

PRAYER

Dear Heavenly Father, help us to guard our hearts and have them focused on the right things—those things that are important to You. In Jesus' name, Amen.

EXPERIENCE
·16·

Don't Break
My Heart

MAIN POINT: Healthy families don't crush each other by expecting perfection.

MATERIALS: Tape measure, painter's tape or sticky notes, chalk, candy bar, broomstick, recorded music, and player. (CD or MP3)

WARM UP

Get a tape measure and **ASK:** "How high do you think you can jump?" Have your child stand next to the wall and stretch his hand up and touch the wall, standing with his feet flat on the floor. Mark the highest point with painter's tape or sticky note.

Coat chalk on his fingertips, and **SAY:** "Now jump as high as you can and touch above the tape." Measure the distance for his vertical leap. Have everyone in the family repeat. Then **SAY:** "I want you to jump 48 inches." Offer a candy bar to the first one who can jump 48 inches. Let them try. They will get frustrated. **ASK:** "Am I being too hard?" Then divide up the candy bar and read the Scripture.

BIBLE READING: Read aloud Colossians 3:21:

Parents, don't come down too hard on your children or you'll crush their spirits. (MSG)

WHAT DOES THE BIBLE SAY?

ASK: "What does this Bible verse mean?" (Parents shouldn't annoy or burden their kids by expecting them to be perfect.) You might have to explain "crush their spirits" as discouragement, or making them sad or feel bad about himself/herself.

ACTIVITY: LIMBO

SAY: "How low can you go?" With a broomstick try to limbo (Bend your back backwards and go underneath the stick without touching it or the floor with your hands). If you are successful, the stick is lowered a notch. This will be frustrating and painful to some parents (who don't bend as well) and fun and entertaining to your kids! Play some Caribbean or Hawaiian music, if you have it. Everybody should try it at least once.

FAMILY DISCUSSION

1. **ASK:** "What was fun with limbo? What was not fun?" (Falling, being in pain, losing)
2. **ASK:** "What would happen if we had to be really good at Limbo or we wouldn't get dessert?" (That would be unfair and frustrating)

WHAT SHOULD WE DO?

1. **ASK:** "Expecting too much from someone can be frustrating to them. It can crush their spirit and discourage them. What are some ways parents are sometimes too hard on their kids?"
2. **ASK:** "Sometimes kids expect their parents to be perfect. Give me an example."

TODAY'S SLOGAN: "Keep it hopeful. Keep it real."

ADAPTING FOR . . .

YOUNGER CHILDREN: Reduce the discussion to two questions. Make sure you explain and illustrate terms that may be too complex for them. For example, in the Bible reading, "don't come down too hard on them," doesn't mean the parents physically squish their kids, but it means they smash their hopes.

TEENS: ASK: "Can teens be too hard on their parents?" "How?" (By expecting too much, or being unrealistic.)

PRAYER

Heavenly Father, help us to be realistic with our expectations of each other and not frustrating. Help us to encourage and support each other. In Jesus' name, Amen.

Heart Training

MAIN POINT: Expecting too little from our kids can frustrate them.

MATERIALS: Wooden blocks or books, containers of soap bubbles (with wands), a pie tin, flex ties (*twisties*), and pipe cleaners.

WARM UP

Holding wooden blocks or books, **SAY:** "I bet nobody can stack these blocks to make a two foot tower?" Allow a child or two to demonstrate, and then **SAY:** "Oh, I guess I was expecting too little of you. How did that make you feel?" (They might say, "Angry, because it was too easy.") (Adjust the height of the tower to accommodate your child's age. If they are 8-10 years, have them try a four-foot tower).

BIBLE READING: Read aloud Ephesians 6:4:

Fathers, do not provoke your children to anger, but bring them up in the discipline and instruction of the Lord. (ESV)

WHAT DOES THE BIBLE SAY?

SAY: "If parents aren't careful, we can make our kids angry and frustrated by how we discipline them. Today's Family Time Experience is about getting the right balance with our training."

ACTIVITY: BUBBLE SCHOOL

Provide a container of bubble soap with a wand for each family member. Pour some of the soap into a pie tin. Make a tiny wand out of flex ties (about ½" in diameter) and another one out of pipe cleaners (About 6" in diameter). **SAY:** "Welcome to Bubble school. Before you open your bubbles, let's do a little research." Ask volunteers to try to blow bubbles using the tiny wand (it won't work too well, if at all). **SAY:** "Perhaps the wand is too small. Let's try the big wand." (Have a few try using the big wand. Unless they are really skilled, this won't work either). **SAY:** "The Bubble Maker knew that most of the time this is the perfect size to make bubbles." Demonstrate how well the wand in the bottle works. Instruct them to open their bubbles and play with them.

FAMILY DISCUSSION

SAY: "Parents are like the right-sized wand. Not too little or not too big. God gave you the right kind of parents that you need to raise you. Children need instruction and discipline. Too little and it won't work. Too much discipline can discourage a child."

WHAT SHOULD WE DO?

1. **ASK:** "What is an example of too little instruction at home, how about at school?"
2. **ASK:** "What might happen if your coach didn't show you anything about playing your sport?"
3. **ASK:** "What is an example of too much discipline at home?"

TODAY'S SLOGAN: "Healthy families are balanced."

ADAPTING FOR . . .

YOUNGER CHILDREN: Skip the Discussion questions and **SAY:** "God made you to be in our family because you fit. We are the right size for you and you are the right size for us. Just like your shoes fit your feet, you fit our family."

TEENS: Reread the Scripture and **ASK:** "What do you think 'approved by the Lord' means?" (Discipline that is based on God's Word, the Bible; and balanced—not too little and not too much.)

PRAYER

Dear Heavenly Father, help us be a balanced family as we train and grow together. In Jesus' name, Amen.

The Last Word

MAIN POINT: The focus of my heart has consequences.

MATERIALS: Play costume clothes for boys and girls, music player, recorded music, pen, and paper.

WARM UP

ASK: "Have you ever had an argument and tried to get in the last word? What is the point of getting in the last word?" (To win the argument.) "Today's Scripture is *God's last word* in the Old Testament. It was followed by 400 years of silence. Listen to what He says:"

BIBLE READING: Read aloud Malachi 4:5-6:

Behold, I will send you Elijah the prophet before the great and awesome day of the LORD comes. And he will turn the hearts of fathers to their children and the hearts of children to their fathers, lest I come and strike the land with a decree of utter destruction. (ESV)

WHAT DOES THE BIBLE SAY?

ASK: "What does it mean to 'turn your heart' toward someone?" (To pay attention, care for, love and think about them, not forget about them.)

ACTIVITY: FORGETFUL FASHION SHOW

Gather some old clothes, hats, scarves, bibs, glasses, costume jewelry, aprons, and other props. **SAY:** "We are going to have a fashion show. Each person gets to put on at least four but not more than seven things and parade in front of us like a fashion show for ten seconds; then leave the room. We will each try to remember what he was wearing."

Play the catwalk music and ham it up!

Have someone record the points for each person with pen and paper. Have the model come back in after each person has tried to remember all that the model was wearing and highlight each prop. Rotate models.

FAMILY DISCUSSION

1. **ASK:** "What helped you remember what they were wearing?"
2. **ASK:** "What did not help you remember?" "What made it hard to remember?"
3. This game required paying attention to other members of the family. **SAY:** "What happens if we don't pay attention to each other in our family?"

TODAY'S SLOGAN: "We experience God's best when we pay attention to each other."

ADAPTING FOR . . .

YOUNGER CHILDREN: Emphasize that we show our caring by paying attention to each other. **ASK:** "What was I wearing yesterday?" or "What did I fix you for breakfast today?"

TEENS: Add these two questions to the Discussion, **ASK:** "Why should parents turn their hearts to their children?" Get responses, then **ASK:** "Why should children turn their hearts to their parents?"

PRAYER

God, there are so many things that grab our attention—that capture our hearts. Help us not be so busy or distracted that we don't connect heart-to-heart. By Your grace, Amen.

·19·

They're Family—
Protect Your Family

MAIN POINT: We can make a difference in one person's life, if we choose to.

MATERIALS: Newspaper, blindfold, trashcan, and *The Blindside* movie

WARM UP

Blind Trashball—Wad up newspaper into balls. Use a towel or bandana as a blindfold. **SAY:** "We are going to see how many of these paper balls we can get in the trash can." (Let everyone shoot.) "Now we are going to see how well we shoot when we can't see." (Blindfold volunteers.) "We have to keep our eyes on the goal if we are going to make it. If we lose sight, we will miss it."

BIBLE READING: Read aloud Psalms 91:14–16.

"Because he loves me," says the LORD, "I will rescue him; I will protect him, for he acknowledges my name. He will call upon me, and I will answer him; I will be with him in trouble, I will deliver him and honor him. With long life I will satisfy him and show him my salvation." (NIV)

ASK: "Most of this Psalm is about protection. What does God promise in this Bible Reading?" (To hear us. To respond, rescue, and protect us.)

ACTIVITY: THE BLINDSIDE

Watch the movie *The Blindside* (The Michael Oher story). If your children are under ten, you may want to break up the movie into two or three nights to watch it.

FAMILY DISCUSSION

1. SAY: "Leigh Anne Tuohy made a huge difference in the life of Michael Oher. Describe some scenes when she did that."
2. ASK: "Healthy families are safe and protect each other. What kind of protection did Michael need?"
3. ASK: "Michael played offensive left tackle—the player on the line with the job to protect the quarterback. Coach Colton had a difficult time explaining this to Michael, until Leigh Ann came out on the field and pointed to the quarterback, halfback, and fullback, and compared them to *his* family at home—The Tuohys. She exclaimed, "They're family. Protect your family!" Then Michael understood and played with passion. "Why is it important to protect your family?""

WHAT SHOULD WE DO?

ASK: "The sacrifice of the Tuohys resulted in unexpected blessings. They took a risk. What are some risks and sacrifices we can make to help someone in need (like Michael)?"

ADAPTING FOR . . .

YOUNGER CHILDREN: Pre-screen the movie and select the key scenes appropriate for your child. Watch the movie at two or three settings. Discuss being safe, protection, care, and love.

TEENS: ASK: "How did Collins Tuohy (the daughter) show love and acceptance for Michael?" **ASK:** "How did Collins take a risk?"

PRAYER

Give us courage to keep our focus on you Lord; to be courageous and willing to stand alone, so that we might finish the race. Amen.

·20·

Live Long and Prosper

MAIN POINT: We must obey the authorities God has placed in our lives.

MATERIALS: A neighborhood park.

WARM UP

ASK: "Is there someone in the world who can say, 'You're not the boss of me'?" (Your child might say the president, or some strong person.) **SAY:** "God is the biggest boss of all. He has helpers who are our bosses or authorities. We have to do what they say. Who are some?" (Teachers, police officers, fire fighters, parents, etc.) "We have to do what these people say to keep us safe and to stay alive."

BIBLE READING: Read aloud Ephesians 6:1–3.

Children, obey your parents in the Lord, for this is right. "Honor your father and mother" (this is the first commandment with a promise), "that it may go well with you and that you may live long in the land." (ESV)

WHAT DOES THE BIBLE SAY?

1. **ASK:** "Obeying parents is the right thing to do because you (the child) *belong* to God. Did you get that? YOU belong to God! You are His! And because you belong to God, He wants us parents to take really good care of you. What do you think about belonging to God?"

2. **ASK:** "What is God's promise for honoring our parents?" (To live a long life, full of blessing.)
3. **ASK:** "What are some ways children can honor their parents?" (Obeying them, talking with respect, etc.)

ACTIVITY/DISCUSSION: PARK WALK

If you live near a neighborhood park, walk to it. Try to use a crosswalk and point out the lines painted on the street. When you get to the park, sit down and . . .

1. **ASK:** "Why did we use the crosswalk?" (Because it's safer. It's the law.)
2. **ASK:** "Why don't we cross wherever we want to?" (Because a car might hit us.) Most parks have rules posted. Point to the sign and **ASK:** "Why do they have rules at a park?"

WHAT SHOULD WE DO?

ASK: "What would happen if they didn't have any rules?" (Dogs would mess up the park; equipment would be broken; cars would be parked on the playground, etc.) **SAY:** "To have fun, we need rules. To live a long life, we have to follow God's rules and obey our parents. That's why, when you were little and I told you to not run into the street you had to obey. Sometimes we don't always see the reason when we are young, but we still have to obey." (After prayer, enjoy the park.)

TODAY'S SLOGAN: "Obeying parents leads to God's best."

ADAPTING FOR . . .

YOUNGER CHILDREN: If the park rules are posted, read the sign to your child and explain the rules. If there isn't a sign, explain some park etiquette to your child. Example: "We take turns."

TEENS: Instead of going to a park, go to batting cages, miniature golf, bumper boats or cars, and have fun. Adapt the Discussion questions to fit. (Example: "What would happen if you ignored the rules at the batting cages?")

PRAYER

Dear Heavenly Father, sometimes it's hard to obey our parents, but we know we will have Your best when we do. Amen.

EXPERIENCE

•21• The Endangered Species

MAIN POINT: Everything I need comes from following the Shepherd.

MATERIALS: Cotton balls, tape, candy, purse, bathrobe, and broomstick.

WARM UP

ASK: "What would it be like to live under the freeway bridge?" (Too noisy, we could never talk; hard to sleep.) **SAY:** "As a family, we need to slow down and not be too busy or too noisy to be with each other, hear each other, and relax together. Rest is almost an *endangered species.*" (You might have to explain that endangered species are animals that are in danger of no longer being around, because only a few of them are alive.)

BIBLE READING: Read aloud Psalm 23:1–3:

> *The Lord is my shepherd; I shall not want. He makes me lie down in green pastures. He leads me beside still waters. He restores my soul. He leads me in paths of righteousness for his name's sake. (ESV)*

WHAT DOES THE BIBLE SAY?

ASK: "What does the shepherd do for the sheep?" (Provide everything they need.)

ACTIVITY: INDOOR SHEPHERDING

Use cotton balls and tape to make each person a "sheep" except you. Tape a ball on the nose and tail of each "sheep." Use a mop or broom as your shepherd's staff. Use an old purse, with a shoulder strap, to hide individually wrapped candies. Wear your bathrobe or a blanket and **SAY:** "I am the shepherd and my sheep follow me." The sheep should "baa baa" and follow you (like Follow the Leader) around on all fours. After a few minutes of following you, **SAY:** "My sheep have everything they need." Guide them into another room where you have secretly hidden some of the candies beforehand. See if they can find them as they graze. **SAY:** "The shepherd lets his sheep rest." Have them pretend to sleep. **SAY:** "He leads them beside peaceful streams." Guide them into the bathroom and turn on the water in the bathtub. **SAY:** "The shepherd renews their strength with food." (Toss each sheep a candy). **SAY:** "The shepherd guides his sheep away from danger and along the *right* paths." Pretend as if you are going to the garage or out the front door, but circle back.

FAMILY DISCUSSION

WHAT SHOULD WE DO?

1. **ASK:** "Why is it important to be a good follower?"
2. **ASK:** "What makes a good shepherd?" (Leader, someone who cares about the sheep, a courageous person.)
3. **ASK:** "Why do we need rest to enjoy each other?" (It takes time to connect.)

TODAY'S SLOGAN: "God is my good shepherd. I can follow Him."

ADAPTING FOR . . .

YOUNGER CHILDREN: The activity will probably work fine with your child, but they may not understand some of the words in the Scripture, so take time to explain them if they don't.

TEENS: Your teen may be too "cool" to pretend he is a little sheep, so switch roles and have your teen be the shepherd and you, and the others be the sheep. If he still won't play along, skip the Activity and lead a Discussion on who are the shepherds of today's teens—the people teens follow and have an allegiance to.

PRAYER

Dear Heavenly Father, thank You that I can trust You to guide me where I'll be safe and that You provide all that I need, because You love me. I will follow You. Amen.

Rest Is a God Idea

MAIN POINT: Resting on Sabbath is God's idea; one we should follow.

MATERIALS: Shoeboxes, construction paper, glue, old magazines, scraps of fabric, and scissors.

WARM UP

ASK: "Where would be a fun place to take a nap? Where would be a really dumb place to take a nap?" **SAY:** "God made us. He knows we need rest. When we don't get enough rest we get grumpy and we don't get along with each other.

BIBLE READING: Read aloud Genesis 2:2–3:

And on the seventh day God finished his work that he had done, and he rested on the seventh day from all his work that he had done. So God blessed the seventh day and made it holy, because on it God rested from all his work that he had done in creation. (ESV)

WHAT DOES THE BIBLE SAY?

ASK: "Why do you think God rested, was He tired?" (No, it was more of an example for us to follow.)

ACTIVITY: SHOEBOX BEDS

Use shoeboxes and construction paper to make miniature beds. Working in pairs, make a headboard and footboard out of construction paper. Glue scraps of fabric on the top of the lid as a bedspread and decorate the sides, both inside and outside with cutouts of magazine photos showing people resting or having fun. Each pair should copy today's Scripture on a piece of paper and glue it inside the box lid. When the beds are finished, have each team share, and describe their pictures. **SAY:** "As we think of other ideas on how to rest, let's write them down and put them in our Shoebox Beds."

FAMILY DISCUSSION

WHAT SHOULD WE DO?

1. **ASK:** "When do you feel most rested?" "When do you wish you could get some rest?"
2. **ASK:** "What can we do as a family to make sure we rest together at least once a week?"

TODAY'S SLOGAN: "A happy family is a rested family."

ADAPTING FOR . . .

YOUNGER CHILDREN: Assist your child with the cutting of the paper and fabric. Explain to her that our "seventh day" is the day we attend church and do things that remind us of God and how much He loves us.

TEENS: Brainstorm ideas on how individual family members and the entire family can create time to rest—*margins* in life to recuperate and re-connect with each other. Select the best ideas and place them in the shoebox. Choose one to do for that week.

PRAYER

Dear Heavenly Father, help us to follow Your example and take time to rest. Help us to take time to worship You and make time for each other. In Jesus' name, Amen.

EXPERIENCE
·23·

A Day of Rest

MAIN POINT: We should take one day a week for worship and rest.

MATERIALS: Shoelaces (or twine)

WARM UP

ASK: "What is your favorite day of the week and why?" (Have everyone respond.)

BIBLE READING: Read aloud Exodus 20:8–10:

Remember the Sabbath day, to keep it holy. Six days you shall labor and do all your work, but the seventh day is the Sabbath of the LORD your God. In it you shall do no work: you, nor your son, nor your daughter, nor your male servant, nor your female servant, nor your cattle, nor your stranger who is within your gates. (NKJV)

WHAT DOES THE BIBLE SAY?

ASK: "What do you think of when you hear the word *holy*?"

ACTIVITY: CENTIPEDE

As the family stands single-file, tie each person's shoes to the person in front of them, with the left feet tied to left feet and right feet tied to right feet. (Do not tie the left foot to the right.)

The goal is to get a centipede effect, with legs moving together in motion. Don't rush. Slowly step together, left foot then right. Create some obstacles to go around. **Safety tip:** Have the youngest kids in front of someone who can assist in case of a fall.

FAMILY DISCUSSION

WHAT SHOULD WE DO?

1. **ASK:** "What did we learn by doing *Centipede?*" (I noticed that . . . we have to go slow and work together; we can't leave anyone out, etc.) Let kids identify their own learning, not a single correct answer.

2. **ASK:** "How did we get around the obstacles?" (By talking and working together.)

3. **ASK:** "*Holy* means 'to set apart, be special, and not like everything else.' If we set aside a day for Sabbath and make it special, we do different things on that day. What are some things we do to remember God on our holy day?"

4. **ASK:** "If we are too busy, we miss time with God and each other. Worship and spending time together as a family are important to God. What happens if we don't make time for each other? For God?"

TODAY'S SLOGAN: "We work together. We rest together. We worship together."

ADAPTING FOR . . .

YOUNGER CHILDREN: Make the obstacles simple and the course short.

TEENS: Make the course more difficult and longer. Deepen the Discussion, and **ASK:** "What are some things we should stop doing in order to have more time for God and for one another?" **ASK:** "What are some things we could do together on our day of rest?"

PRAYER

Dear Heavenly Father, Thank You for Your example of taking time for worship—You deserve our praise. Thank You for Your example of taking time for rest—we need it. Amen.

EXPERIENCE

•24•

Only One Thing Is Needed

MAIN POINT: Sometimes tasks can take us away from what is most important.

MATERIALS: A sturdy kitchen chair.

WARM UP

ASK: "If we have a guest in our home would you rather sit with him and listen to his stories, or would you rather help get the meal ready? Why?"

BIBLE READING: Read aloud Luke 10:38–42:

> *Now it happened as they went that He entered a certain village; and a certain woman named Martha welcomed Him into her house. And she had a sister called Mary, who also sat at Jesus' feet and heard His word. But Martha was distracted with much serving, and she approached Him and said, "Lord, do You not care that my sister has left me to serve alone? Therefore tell her to help me." And Jesus answered and said to her, "Martha, Martha, you are worried and troubled about many things. But one thing is needed, and Mary has chosen that good part, which will not be taken away from her." (NKJV)*

FAMILY DISCUSSION

WHAT DOES THE BIBLE SAY?

1. **ASK:** "Do you think Mary was being lazy by not helping her sister?"

2. **ASK:** "Why didn't Jesus tell Mary to go help Martha?"

ASK: "Some people are more *Doers* while others are *Relaters*. Martha was a *Doer*—she was all about getting the task done. Mary was a *Relater*—she was interested in people and didn't pay attention to the work. Which are you?"

ACTIVITY: CHAIR LIFT

SAY: "There is a time to talk and a time for tasks; but if we work together, the task is easier AND we can talk." Have someone sit in a sturdy kitchen chair. Ask each person to try to lift the seated person and the chair. **SAY:** "By yourself this task is too difficult; but let's try it together." Have the entire family lift the person and the chair a few inches off the floor. **SAY:** "Many hands make the work light."

TODAY'S SLOGAN: "People come before things."

ADAPTING FOR . . .

YOUNGER CHILDREN: Adjust the vocabulary in Discussion question 3 to, "Who are you more like in the story, Martha (who was busy in the kitchen) or Mary (who sat at Jesus' feet)?" If your children are too young to help lift a person, instead of a person, try using phone books, dictionaries, and books.

TEENS: Develop the idea of *Doers* and *Relaters* and **ASK:** "What situations call for more of a *Doer* mentality? What situations are more suited for a *Relater*?"

PRAYER

Dear Father, help us to know when to talk and when to work. We want to be the kind of family that helps each other with difficult tasks. Thank You for the strength we have together. Amen.

EXPERIENCE
•25•

The Luxury of Sitting

MAIN POINT: We need to be willing to stop, listen, and serve each other.

MATERIALS: A bucket, washcloths, towel, warm water with a little soap in it, a chair, and perfume.

WARM UP

ASK: "What is your favorite smell? Would you buy a perfume of this smell?"

BIBLE READING: Read aloud John 12:3:

Mary therefore took a pound of expensive ointment made from pure nard, and anointed the feet of Jesus and wiped his feet with her hair. The house was filled with the fragrance of the perfume. (ESV)

ACTIVITY: FEET WASHING

Prepare a bucket with warm water and a little soap in it, washcloths, towel, and a chair. **SAY:** "Mary did more than the usual custom of the time of washing the feet of your house guests; she sat at the Jesus' feet to listen and learn from Him. Then she took out some expensive perfume—worth a whole year's pay—and sprinkled it all over Jesus' feet. In Jesus' time, they wore sandals and their feet got dirty because they had to walk everywhere. They didn't have cars then. So today we are going to wash each other's feet." Take turns washing each other's feet. Pat them dry, and then sprinkle them with some cologne or perfume.

FAMILY DISCUSSION

WHAT SHOULD WE DO?

1. ASK: "How did it feel to have someone wash your feet?"
2. ASK: "Which did you like better: washing or having your feet washed?"
3. ASK: "Washing feet was appreciated in Bible times because people had dirty, tired feet from walking. Today, we have other needs that still require us to serve others. Sometimes it might mean that we stop what we are doing, and listen to the other person in our family. Would this be easy or hard for you? Why?"

TODAY'S SLOGAN: "Sometimes the best gift is time."

ADAPTING FOR . . .

YOUNGER CHILDREN: Go through the activity and discussion quickly; otherwise your little one may be tempted to play in the water. Remove the water for the discussion.

TEENS: ASK: "When Mary put perfume on Jesus' feet it was considered extravagant, even scandalous because 'good' women weren't supposed to touch men's feet like that. Why do you think Mary took the risk to do this? What was she trying to show?"

PRAYER

Lord, help us to make time for each other and to look for ways to serve each other. Amen.

EXPERIENCE
•26•

Favorites

MAIN POINT: Playing favorites is hurtful.

MATERIALS: *Toy Story* movie, popcorn, and bowls.

WARM UP

Gather the family and two bowls and **SAY:** "We are going to watch a movie and have popcorn, but we only have enough for two people—me (take a bowl) and someone else (hold it up). Who should it be?" After a few minutes of mayhem, chose someone, then to the others, **ASK:** "How do you feel about this?" (Unfair, playing favorites.) **SAY:** "Actually, I was just trying to illustrate the point. You all will get popcorn, and your own bowls. Today we are talking about playing favorites—not being fair."

BIBLE READING: Read aloud James 3:16–17.

Whenever you're trying to look better than others or get the better of others, things fall apart and everyone ends up at the other's throats. Real wisdom, God's wisdom, begins with a holy life and is characterized by getting along with others. It is gentle and reasonable, overflowing with mercy and blessings, not hot one day and cold the next, not two-faced. (MSG)

WHAT DOES THE BIBLE SAY?

ASK: "What happens when we try to show off and look better than someone else?" (It leads to problems.)

ACTIVITY: MOVIE NIGHT—TOY STORY

Pop some popcorn and get comfy for a fun movie. Take a few minutes to discuss at the end.

FAMILY DISCUSSION

ASK: "Who said, 'They'll see. I'm still Andy's favorite toy.' What happened?"

WHAT SHOULD WE DO?

1. ASK: "What happens when people play favorites?" "How did this happen in the movie?"
2. ASK: "What helped patch things up in the end?"
3. ASK: "What can we learn from this movie?"

TODAY'S SLOGAN: "Being real and fair is smart."

ADAPTING FOR . . .

YOUNGER CHILDREN: If they are tired or restless, you may want to watch the movie in two settings.

TEENS: ASK: "What are some ways you see people play favorites at school? On the athletic field? With friends?"

PRAYER

Dear God, help us to be fair with our friends and family. This is the smart way to live. Amen.

EXPERIENCE
·27·

Be Wise

MAIN POINT: We should be content with what we have.

MATERIALS: Construction paper, tape, scissors, and markers.

WARM UP

ASK: "What are some things that we as parents and kids sometimes whine or complain about?" Write these on a large piece of paper.

BIBLE READING: Read aloud James 3:13–16.

If you are wise and understand God's ways, prove it by living an honorable life, doing good works with the humility that comes from wisdom. But if you are bitterly jealous and there is selfish ambition in your heart, don't cover up the truth with boasting and lying. For jealousy and selfishness are not God's kind of wisdom. Such things are earthly, unspiritual, and demonic. For wherever there is jealousy and selfish ambition, there you will find disorder and evil of every kind. (NLT)

WHAT DOES THE BIBLE SAY?

ASK: "If you whine about what you don't have, does it make you feel better or change anything?" (No.) "So, how do we keep from whining? That is today's lesson."

FAMILY DISCUSSION

ASK: "Why does wanting something that belongs to someone else cause problems?" (It can lead to envy or stealing)

WHAT SHOULD WE DO?
ASK: "How does being selfish (not sharing) create problems?"

ACTIVITY: PRAYER CHAIN

Using strips of construction paper, tape, and markers, make links of things you are thankful for and content with having. This is an anti-jealousy prescription. Each person should write or draw a description of at least five things, then link them together, alternating from person to person. You could also add his or her name to each link. Try to make your chain at least six feet long. Display it in a prominent place in your home. **OPTION:** Have each person use a different color paper so he or she can find their own in the chain to reaffirm their own thoughts.

TODAY'S SLOGAN: "Contentment is a choice."

ADAPTING FOR . . .

YOUNGER CHILDREN: Reduce the links of contentment to three each for your child.

TEENS: ASK: "How does jealousy and selfish ambition lead to disorder and evil?" Give an example using teens.

PRAYER

We are thankful to You Lord for the many things You have given us: our home, our health, our family; but most of all Your Son and new life in Him. Help us to be content with all of these wonderful gifts of grace. In Jesus' name, Amen.

EXPERIENCE

•28•

Audience of One

MAIN POINT: We should do good deeds for God's approval, not people's.

MATERIALS: Groceries for sack lunch, ingredients to make cookies, or a gift card for groceries.

WARM UP

ASK: "What do you think about those kids at school who get a good grade, then parade it around, showing it off?" **ASK:** "What about those football players who show off in the end zone after making a touchdown? Too much show?"

BIBLE READING: Read aloud Matthew 6:1–4.

> Watch out! Don't do your good deeds publicly, to be admired by others, for you will lose the reward from your Father in heaven. When you give to someone in need, don't do as the hypocrites do—blowing trumpets in the synagogues and streets to call attention to their acts of charity! I tell you the truth, they have received all the reward they will ever get. But when you give to someone in need, don't let your left hand know what your right hand is doing. Give your gifts in private, and your Father, who sees everything, will reward you. (NLT)

WHAT DOES THE BIBLE SAY?

ASK: "Why do these fake lovers of God (hypocrites) like to show off in front of others?" (So others will be impressed with them).

ACTIVITY: STEALTH SERVICE

1. **ASK:** "Think of someone in our community who is needy. They could be homeless, out of work, discouraged, sad because of a loss, or facing a life-threatening illness."

2. **ASK:** "What could *we* do to encourage and help this person?" (Make a sack lunch for the homeless; send a card with a grocery gift card to encourage others; bake cookies and visit someone for a short time. Decide what to do and carry out your mission, but keep it top secret!)

3. **ASK:** "Who will read today's Bible reading again, aloud?"

FAMILY DISCUSSION: (AFTER THE STEALTH SERVICE)

1. **ASK:** "What did you think about doing the *Stealth Service?*"

2. **ASK:** "What changed after we served?" (Started to think of others.)

3. **ASK:** "Why did Jesus say not to call attention to yourself when you serve?"(Because your only reward is others noticing what you've done.)

TODAY'S SLOGAN: "We live for an audience of One."

ADAPTING FOR . . .

YOUNGER CHILDREN: Change the Warm-up question to, "What's wrong with being a 'tattle-tale'?" (You are trying to get someone else in trouble and make yourself look good.) You will also need to explain the slogan. Try "God sees all that we do. We should be more concerned with what He thinks, than what people think."

TEENS: Brainstorm several ways you could do service and make it "stealth." Write down the ideas and select one. The other ideas could be used later. Teens will like the stealth element of the activity. Also, deepen the Discussion, **ASK:** "Can you imagine *tooting your own horn*—actually blowing a trumpet when you did a good deed? Why is this so obnoxious?"

PRAYER

Dear Heavenly Father, help us to serve others without expecting payback or attention on us. Teach us to only seek Your reward. Amen.

EXPERIENCE

•29•

Recharge

MAIN POINT: Everybody needs time to recharge.

MATERIALS: Battery-powered toy or tool, nutrition bars, and sports drinks.

WARM UP

Hold up a battery powered toy or tool. Turn it on and **ASK:** "What happens if I leave this on for a long time, like overnight?" (The battery will go dead.) **SAY:** "Today we learn we need to recharge too when we get tired, just like this rechargeable battery."

BIBLE READING: Read aloud Luke 5:15–16.

But despite Jesus' instructions, the report of his power spread even faster, and vast crowds came to hear him preach and to be healed of their diseases. But Jesus often withdrew to the wilderness for prayer. (NLT)

WHAT DOES THE BIBLE SAY?

ASK: "Why did Jesus sometimes pull away from the crowds?" (For prayer.)

FAMILY DISCUSSION

ASK: "What makes you tired or feel worn-out?"

WHAT SHOULD WE DO?

1. **ASK:** "What helps you get your strength back (recharge)?" (Take a nap.)

2. **ASK:** "God told us to recharge every week by keeping the Sabbath and worshipping Him rather than working on that day. Why is this so important?" (To focus on him; renew our relationships; rest.)

3. **ASK:** "Jesus didn't always meet the demands of the crowds. He knew he needed time alone to pray to renew His strength. How does prayer give us strength?" (Makes us feel connected with God—our source of strength.)

ACTIVITY: HIKE 'N' SNACK

Get one nutrition bar and one sports drink per person. Put on comfortable walking shoes and go on a hike. Make it appropriate for the age of your youngest child. Midway, stop, sit down, and have your drink and snack and **ASK:** "Did that recharge you? Did you get more energy from the bar and the drink?" Take a few answers, then **SAY:** "We need to do the same thing every week—we need to take a break for rest and worship." Then finish the hike.

TODAY'S SLOGAN: "Everybody needs to recharge."

ADAPTING FOR . . .

YOUNGER CHILDREN: ASK: "What happens when you don't get a nap?" For the Activity: keep the hike short, maybe only fifteen minutes total.

TEENS: ASK: "In some of the sports you've participated in, or observed recently, how do the athletes rest and catch their breath in the middle of the game?"

PRAYER

Thank You God for our bodies and rest and how You renew us every morning. In Jesus' name, Amen.

Who's Kingdom Is It?

MAIN POINT: I want to advance God's kingdom, not mine.

MATERIALS: Individually wrapped candies, an ice cream scoop, a large bowl, and a blindfold.

WARM UP

ASK: "Why does a basketball coach or soccer coach have to watch the game? Why can't she hang out at the snack bar?" (Because she has to watch the game and tell the players what to do to play better.) **SAY:** "God is like a coach—to live right we need to listen to Him."

BIBLE READING: Read aloud Matthew 6:9–11:

> *In this manner, therefore, pray: Our father in heaven, hallowed be Your name. Your kingdom come. Your will be done on earth as it is in heaven. Give us this day our daily bread. (NKJV)*

WHAT DOES THE BIBLE SAY?

ASK: "What do you think of when you think of a *kingdom*?"

ACTIVITY: SWEET SCOOPS

Get some individually wrapped candies (like Hershey's *Kisses*), an ice cream scoop, a large plastic bowl, and a blindfold. Sit in a circle on the carpet or rug. Randomly spread ten of the kisses on the floor. Select one child and blindfold him or her, and **SAY:** "You have thirty seconds to collect the candy, but you have to do it blindfolded and with one arm behind your back. You can only pick them up with the scoop. You get to keep the ones that get in the bowl. Go!" Have everyone else count slowly to thirty. He may only get a few in. When time is up, **SAY:** "Now let's do this with help. Listen to your guide for directions." (Choose one volunteer.) Repeat the process, this time with the guide verbally directing the "blind" volunteer. Take turns. Share the candy.

FAMILY DISCUSSION

WHAT SHOULD WE DO?

SAY: "We advance God's kingdom by letting Him rule areas of our lives. We don't always know how to do this at first. We grow by turning over each area for His will to be done in it."

1. **ASK:** "What was the difference between doing it by yourself and having a guide?"
2. **ASK:** "Was it more fun with a guide?"
3. **ASK:** "God is our guide and we need to listen to Him, even though it may not be exactly what we want—He sees things we don't see. Give me an example."

TODAY'S SLOGAN: "God's kingdom is where He rules."

ADAPTING FOR . . .

YOUNGER CHILDREN: Don't spread out the candy too far from them. If they have difficulty, allow them to use the hand (which was behind their back) to help them find the candy.

TEENS: Add a couple of dollar bills crumpled up into balls. Allow them to see these before they are blindfolded. **ASK:**

"Doing God's will may go against what a teen might want to do? Can you think of a few examples?" ("Doing what my parents say, even though I think it's dumb.")

PRAYER

Help me God to trust in You and let You be in charge of my life, especially when I want to be the boss. Amen.

EXPERIENCE
•31•

May I Serve You?

MAIN POINT: Learning to give can be fun and rewarding.

MATERIALS: Transportation to the dollar store, one-dollar and one dime for each family member, pen and paper.

WARM UP

SAY: "Please describe a time when you gave a gift to someone and they really liked it."

BIBLE READING: Read aloud Acts 20:35.

And I have been a constant example of how you can help those in need by working hard. You should remember the words of the Lord Jesus: 'It is more blessed to give than to receive.'" (NLT)

WHAT DOES THE BIBLE SAY?

ASK: "Why would giving make someone happy?"

ACTIVITY: CHEAP SHOPPING SPREE

Give each person one dollar (and a dime for tax, if needed). Go to a dollar store, or any store that has a selection of one-dollar items. **SAY:** "Each of us is going to buy a secret-just-for-fun gift for someone else in our family." (Draw names for the assignments.) "Your job is to find something that is a perfect fit for the person, or is silly, useful, or just plain fun! You will have fifteen minutes to shop. We will meet in front of the store in fifteen minutes and wrap the gifts at home. Keep it a secret!"

FAMILY DISCUSSION

Back home after you have opened the wrapped gifts. (You might want to buy a cheap snack to share.)

1. **ASK:** "Did you have fun shopping?"
2. **ASK:** Read aloud the Scripture and **ASK:** "What does it mean to be blessed?" "Why is blessing (through giving) better than receiving?"
3. **ASK:** "How did you feel when your person opened their gift?"

TODAY'S SLOGAN: "The real joy in living is giving."

ADAPTING FOR . . .

YOUNGER CHILDREN: A parent or older child should accompany younger children in the store. If you have more than one younger child, take turns buying the gifts. You will need to help your preschooler choose a gift and wrap it at home. But remind them it is a secret!

TEENS: **ASK:** "What are some other gifts—the kind you don't have to buy—that we can give each other in our family?" If needed, for the store outing, ask your teen to accompany a younger sibling.

PRAYER

Teach us Father that it is more blessed to give than to receive. Help us to see when we can do that every day. Amen.

Holding Things Loosely

MAIN POINT: All that we have can fall apart, break or be stolen.

MATERIALS: Drawing paper, markers or crayons, a shoebox or small cardboard box, brown or black construction paper, glue, rope, bangles, and small knickknacks from around the house. Optional: thin strips of balsa wood.

WARM UP

ASK: "What is your most prized possession? Your favorite thing in all the world?"

BIBLE READING: Read aloud Matthew 6:19–21:

Do not lay up for yourselves treasures on earth, where moth and rust destroy and where thieves break in and steal; but lay up for yourselves treasures in heaven, where neither moth nor rust destroys and where thieves do not break in and steal. For where your treasure is, there your heart will be also. (NKJV)

WHAT DOES THE BIBLE SAY?

ASK: "What is a treasure?" (Something that is worth a lot, either in money or in memories. We think about our treasures, they are important to us.)

ACTIVITY: TREASURE CHEST

Build a treasure chest out of a box with brown or black construction paper glued to the sides. (You could also use thin strips of balsa wood, glued to the box). Decorate with knickknacks found around the house (hardware, rope, bangles, etc.). Have each person draw two or three pictures of their favorite things: toys, clothes, food, entertainment, etc. and place these in the chest. SAY: "We need to hide the treasure chest in a safe place, you stay here while I do that. No peeking." Hide it in a challenging, but not impossible place. Then have your children look for it. If you have time, repeat the process with the finder hiding it.

FAMILY DISCUSSION

After you find the chest . . .

WHAT SHOULD WE DO?

1. **ASK:** "Even though we hid our favorite treasures, they can be destroyed by rust or moths or thieves could steal them. How would you feel if someone actually stole your favorite thing?"

2. **ASK:** "If we spend most of our time doing things that please God, we don't have so much time to pile up the things that might be lost, stolen, or damaged. God's rewards are mothproof, rustproof, and thief-proof. What pleases God?"

3. **ASK:** "If our heart is always thinking about our stuff, it shows that our treasure *is* stuff. But if we are thinking about love, kindness, sharing, and being thankful, these are the treasures that last. Why are those so valuable?"

TODAY'S SLOGAN: "Your treasure is what is on your heart."

ADAPTING FOR . . .

YOUNGER CHILDREN: This is a fairly abstract lesson, so bring the concepts down to concrete terms your child will understand. For example, **SAY:** "You treasure is your most valuable thing, it could be a toy, a doll, your favorite dress, your scooter, etc."

Don't make the hiding place too high or too hard for your preschooler.

TEENS: Help your teen make a break from all the materialistic hype that surrounds him or her. **ASK:** "Do you realize that everything that you own is susceptible to being stolen, falling apart, or someone breaking it? If that's the case, what should our view be toward owning stuff?" (Hold our possessions loosely. All of our stuff really belongs to God, He's just loaned it to us.)

PRAYER

Dear Heavenly Father, Help my attention to be on You and the things of Your kingdom. Help me to grow past wanting only the things of earth to wanting the true treasures. In Jesus' name, Amen.

EXPERIENCE
·33·

Love Is
on the Inside

MAIN POINT: True love looks beyond the looks.

MATERIALS: Popcorn, *Shrek 2* movie, old magazines, and scissors.

WARM UP

Clip some pictures from magazines or newspapers of various kinds of people: strong, good-looking, happy, sad, weak, mad, etc. Hold these up, one at a time, and **ASK:** "What do you think about this person? What kind of person is she/he? What kind of mood is she/he in? Would you like this person to be your friend?"

BIBLE READING: Read aloud 1 Samuel 16:7:

> But the LORD said to Samuel, "Do not look on his appearance or on the height of his stature, because I have rejected him. For the LORD sees not as man sees: man looks on the outward appearance, but the LORD looks on the heart." *(ESV)*

WHAT DOES THE BIBLE SAY?

ASK: "What does it mean to judge someone?" (Decide if they are good or bad by looking at their outside, not their inside.)

ACTIVITY: SHREK 2

Pop some popcorn and get comfortable for a great family movie.

FAMILY DISCUSSION

WHAT SHOULD WE DO?

1. **ASK:** "How did Shrek demonstrate that true love looks beyond the looks?"
2. **ASK:** "What qualities did Shrek show that you liked (courage, loyalty, sense of humor)?"
3. **ASK:** "What are some ways we can show true love by going beyond just the looks?"

TODAY'S SLOGAN: "Love looks deeper than the looks."

ADAPTING FOR . . .

YOUNGER CHILDREN: Try showing the movie on Saturday or Sunday afternoon or early enough in the evening so it doesn't keep your preschooler up past his bedtime. Or consider showing in two screenings.

TEENS: This is one family movie that teens will watch more than once. Extend the Discussion and **ASK:** "What romantic themes did you see in the movie?" "What was unusual about Fiona and Shrek falling in love?"

PRAYER

Father God, thank You that Your love is true and goes beyond the looks. We praise You for how You loved us, even when we weren't so lovable. Amen.

EXPERIENCE
·34·

Life Is Worship

MAIN POINT: All of life is worship.

MATERIALS: Pen, paper, plastic grocery bags, a roll of clear contact paper, crayons, scissors, and stuff from nature to be collected (leaves, sticks, buds, etc.).

WARM UP

ASK: "When is a good time to pray?" (Before meals, before tests at school, before bedtime, all the time.)

BIBLE READING: Read aloud Matthew 6:32b–33:

Your heavenly Father already knows all your needs. Seek the Kingdom of God above all else, and live righteously, and he will give you everything you need. (NLT)

WHAT DOES THE BIBLE SAY?

ASK: "What will God, our heavenly Father give us?" (All of our needs, not wants.)

FAMILY DISCUSSION

WHAT SHOULD WE DO?

1. **ASK:** "What are some of our daily needs?" (List them.)
2. **ASK:** "How does God meet our daily needs?"

3. **ASK:** "When you look at the beauty of God's creation; what are you thankful for?" (Sky, trees, lakes, birds, etc.; list them)

ACTIVITY: PRAISE EXPEDITION

Get outside to a park or a place that has lots of trees and natural beauty. Bring your lists of daily needs and what you are thankful for, along with a plastic grocery bag for each person. You are on an expedition to collect things that remind you of God and how He provides for you. Spend ten minutes collecting the material and then sit down at a picnic table or return home with your findings to make *Praise Mats* (Placemats of Praise). Using the leaves and other natural findings, along with crayon drawings illustrating how God provides, or what we like in nature, you will each make a placemat using clear contact paper. Cut the roll of contact paper into 11" x 17" pieces, place the drawings and natural objects on it, and then cover with another piece of clear contact paper. You may want to include today's Scripture or slogan on the *Praise Mat*.

TODAY'S SLOGAN: "Hug each minute as a gift from God."

ADAPTING FOR . . .

YOUNGER CHILDREN: Help your child collect the leaves and nature materials. Pre-cut the contact paper, help her place on the sticky surface, and cover with the second layer of contact paper. She may need help in writing her name or other words that she wants for her Praise Mat.

TEENS: Encourage them to pick a quality of God as a theme for their Praise Mat, such as "grace" or "amazing" or "light," and find elements of nature to illustrate it. They may also draw or paint scenes for their Praise Mat. In that case, you will need watercolor paints or markers.

PRAYER

Dear Heavenly Father, help us to see You in each part of our lives—our family, our friends, at school, in our neighborhood and in the beautiful scenes of nature. There is so much to praise You for! Praise Your Name! Amen.

EXPERIENCE ·35·

Bringing It Home

> **MAIN POINT:** Passing on good values takes practice.
>
> **MATERIALS:** Ten pennies per child, a muffin tin, masking tape, marker, pen, and paper. Optional: Cupcakes as a treat.

WARM UP

ASK: "If you spend the night in the garage does that make you a car? Why not? How about if you spend the night in a fire station, does that make you a firefighter? Why not?" (Because you have to do things on purpose, not just by accident. Like learning to ride a bike, you have to practice—not just look at it or think about it.)

BIBLE READING: Read aloud 2 Corinthians 8:11:

> *Now you should finish what you started. Let the eagerness you showed in the beginning be matched now by your giving. Give in proportion to what you have. (NLT)*

WHAT DOES THE BIBLE SAY?

ASK: "Describe a time when you finished something that was hard to finish."

ACTIVITY: KITCHEN KARNIVAL

Gather ten pennies per child; a muffin tin with each cup

numbered 1-12 with masking tape. **SAY:** "Welcome to Kitchen Karnival! We are going to play a game of tossing our pennies into the muffin tin. The goal is to get the highest score. Each cup has a value, 1-12. We will go one at a time. You have to stand behind this line when you toss." (Make a line on the floor with masking tape.) "Before we start, let me demonstrate. Now watch carefully."

Throw ALL of your ten pennies at once toward or near the muffin tin. You aren't trying to get them in. They will laugh. **ASK:** "What's wrong with this?" (Too random; need to aim; try one at a time.) **SAY:** "That's right. To be successful, we have to aim—one goal at a time." Let each child have a turn. Add up the score. **SAY:** "We are all winners" and serve cupcakes to all. Give two cupcakes to the actual winner.

FAMILY DISCUSSION

WHAT SHOULD WE DO?

1. **SAY:** "Sometimes it's helpful to break a big project down into 'bite-size' pieces. It's like that old joke, 'How do you eat an elephant? One bite at a time!' Why were we more successful at throwing one penny at a time?"
2. **ASK:** "Passing on good values and helping you to learn to be a good person takes practice. It takes repeating little things over and over. What are some of those?" (Brushing teeth, being kind to each other, cleaning up our own messes.)
3. **ASK:** "What is a 'habit'? Is it good or bad?" (Both.) "Is it enough to say you are going to do something?" (No, you need to follow through and do it.)

TODAY'S SLOGAN: "It won't happen by accident."

ADAPTING FOR . . .

YOUNGER CHILDREN: Make the toss line closer to the muffin tin. Try about three feet away. Help them add up the score.

TEENS: Move the toss line further away from the muffin tin. If you have teens and younger kids, make two toss lines using the masking tape; with the kids' line about four to five feet away from the tin, and the teens' at six feet away. Extend the Discussion and **ASK:** "What habits produce success for teens?" (Study habits, health habits, finishing difficult projects.)

PRAYER

Father God, help us to follow through on the things we say are important. Help us to not give up, but to keep practicing. Amen.

EXPERIENCE

•36•

No Fear

MAIN POINT: We can give our fear to the Lord.

MATERIALS: *Soul Surfer* movie and popcorn.

WARM UP

ASK: "What do you dream of doing someday?" **SAY:** "Today we are going to see a movie about Bethany Hamilton, who always dreamed of being a pro surfer, but something got in the way."

BIBLE READING: Read aloud 2 Timothy 1:7:

> *For God gave us a spirit not of fear, but of power and love and self-control. (ESV)*

WHAT DOES THE BIBLE SAY?

ASK: "When we are afraid, God is with us and will give us strength. What are you afraid of?"

ACTIVITY: SOUL SURFER MOVIE

(The shark attack scene is pretty mild and not graphic. But you may choose to skip it. It's in Chapter Five.)

FAMILY DISCUSSION

WHAT SHOULD WE DO?

1. **ASK:** "How did Bethany's family and friends support her?"

2. **SAY:** "From a very young age, Bethany wanted to be a pro surfer. It was her dream and passion. The shark attack smashed those dreams and she discovered that it was very difficult to compete. At *regionals* she suffered a broken board and a crushed spirit. She gave her board away and quit competing. Do you ever feel broken and feel like quitting?"

3. **SAY:** Bethany went with her youth group to serve in tsunami-ravaged Thailand. She teaches a kid to surf. Bethany narrates, "They say the Lord works in mysterious ways. I say that's an understatement. Who would have thought that teaching a kid to surf would teach me that surfing isn't the most important thing in the world and that something else is—love? Bigger than any tidal wave, more powerful than any fear." **ASK:** "Why is love more powerful than fear?"

4. **ASK:** "How did love help Bethany recapture her confidence and get back to surfing in competitions?"

TODAY'S SLOGAN: "Love conquers fear."

ADAPTING FOR . . .

YOUNGER CHILDREN: Skip the shark attack scene (Chapter 5) and maybe some of the hospital scenes, for children younger than eight years old.

TEENS: ASK: "How did Bethany's family and friends deal with her doubt?" **ASK:** "Bethany had a supportive youth group leader, friends, and family. How does a supportive community help us in tragedy?" For more discussion on this outstanding movie, check out the free, downloadable Family Studies @ http://www.soulsurferwave.com/familybiblestudies.

PRAYER

Father God, thank You that You do not give us a spirit of fear, but of power and love and self-control—even when very scary things happen to us. We can have confidence in Your strength and presence. Amen.

EXPERIENCE
·37· A Peaceful Family

> **MAIN POINT:** Stress is feeling out of control. Peace is realizing God is in control.
>
> **MATERIALS:** Two small *Ziploc*® bags, a wire coat hanger, masking tape, pen, and fifty pennies.

WARM UP

ASK: "When have you been stressed or worried?"

BIBLE READING: Read aloud John 14:27:

I am leaving you with a gift—peace of mind and heart. And the peace I give is a gift the world cannot give. So don't be troubled or afraid. (NLT)

WHAT DOES THE BIBLE SAY?

ASK: "Where does peace come from?" (Jesus.)

ACTIVITY: PEACE HANGS IN THE BALANCE

Gather the materials and label the plastic bags with masking tape: *Stress & Worry* on one, and *God's Control/Truth* on the other. Place a penny in each bag and zip the bags on the bottom of the clothes hanger (as far as it will zip) with each bag balancing the other.

1. **SAY:** "Write something you are worried about on masking

tape with one abbreviated word or drawing, place on a penny, and place in *Worry* bag.

2. **SAY:** "Try to think of a truth you know about God and how He is in control. Write it on tape and stick it to a penny and put in the *Truth* bag."

3. Have each person do three or more worries and three or more truths. **SAY:** "Peace is balancing our stress and worries with God's truth and remembering that He is in control of the details of our life."

FAMILY DISCUSSION

WHAT SHOULD WE DO?

1. **ASK:** "Do all people worry?" (Yes, even adults.)
2. **SAY:** "Why is personal peace important?" (Because without it, we get stressed out.)
3. **ASK:** "Why do we need peace in our family?" (So we can relax together and deal with worries.)

TODAY'S SLOGAN: "I can have peace because I know God is in control."

ADAPTING FOR . . .

YOUNGER CHILDREN: You will need to help them symbolize their worries and list for them some of God's truths (God is loving; God is everywhere; God knows all things, etc.), and help them illustrate the quality about God, or write the word for them.

TEENS: ASK: "How can remembering that God is in control of even the details of my life bring peace?" (If you have too many worries, the baggie may fall from the hanger. Try using tape to hold it on.) ASK: "What can we do to discover and remember truths about God?" (To balance the fears and worries?) (Read God's Word; attend Bible studies; worship; listen to music that focuses on God; journal; pray; be in community with other followers of Christ.)

PRAYER

Father God, help us to experience Your peace—the kind that is greater than our understanding. Peace that calms our worried hearts. In Jesus' name, Amen.

EXPERIENCE
•38•
A Truthful Family

MAIN POINT: Healthy families are truthful.

MATERIALS: Twine or yarn, chair, and scissors.

WARM UP

ASK: "For relationships to be healthy and strong, they have to be based on truth. People have problems when they believe things that are not true. Can you think of some fairy tales and stories when people believed things that weren't true? What are some? What problems did they cause? (e.g., *The Emperor's New Clothes*—he paraded naked (the fable by Hans Christian Anderson)! In *Cinderella*, she believed she was worthless because her wicked stepmother told her she was.)

SCRIPTURE READING: Read aloud Ephesians 4:15:

Rather, speaking the truth in love, we are to grow up in every way into him who is the head, into Christ. (ESV)

WHAT DOES THE BIBLE SAY?

ASK: "We are to tell the truth because it is right and the loving thing to do. How would you feel if someone lied about you?" (Not loved.)

ACTIVITY: WEB OF LIES

SAY: "When we lie, it's like being caught in a spider web; it becomes more and more complex and can restrict us." Have a volunteer sit in a simple, straight chair. Secretly whisper to the volunteer, "This is one time when we want you to lie about everything. We are going to take turns asking you questions, and each time, you lie." Have the other children ask him questions: "How old are you?" or "Where do you live?" etc. After each lie, wrap some twine around him and the chair. Do not cut the twine. (Don't make it too tight to cut off circulation. Have scissors handy to cut the twine.) After he is caught in a huge web, explain to the others that you asked him to lie, and that lying gets us into a web of deceit that traps, like a spider web. Go on to Discussion.

FAMILY DISCUSSION

WHAT SHOULD WE DO?

1. **ASK:** "What did you think about the game *Web of Lies*?"
2. To the volunteer "liar," **ASK:** "How did it feel to lie?"
3. To everyone, **ASK:** "What would happen to our family if we really did tell that many lies?" (After the Discussion, be sure to untie the "liar".)

TODAY'S SLOGAN: "We will balance the truth with love."

ADAPTING FOR . . .

YOUNGER CHILDREN: You may have to explain a fairy tale or two to your child. She may not immediately get the connection between fantasy and real life.

TEENS: Deepen the Discussion and explain that myths are beliefs we hold that are familiar but not 100-percent accurate. They *seem* true, but in reality, they are not. They are a common form of deception. **ASK:** "What frees us from the myths and deceptions?" (Truth.) Ask for examples of things we know are solid truth. For each one shared, cut away at a string of deception around the volunteer. **SAY:** "Truth leads to freedom."

PRAYER

Thank You God that You are a God of truth and there is nothing dishonest about You. We can trust You because You are truth. Because of Your truth, we are free. Amen.

Heroes at Home

MAIN POINT: We can be powerful when we stick together.

MATERIALS: *The Incredibles* movie and popcorn.

WARM UP

ASK: "What can you do together that you can't do alone?"

BIBLE READING: Read aloud Joshua 1:7:

> *Only be strong and very courageous, being careful to do accord-ing to all the law that Moses my servant commanded you. Do not turn from it to the right and or to the left, that you may have good success wherever you go.* (ESV)

WHAT DOES THE BIBLE SAY?

ASK: "What do you think about that promise 'you will be suc-cessful wherever you go'?"

ACTIVITY: *THE INCREDIBLES*

Pop some popcorn and enjoy the movie. Save time for discus-sion afterwards.

FAMILY DISCUSSION

1. **ASK:** "How were the Parrs different from our family?" (They have superpowers.)
2. **ASK:** "Violet and Dash wanted to fit in and be normal

at the beginning of the movie, but towards the end, while they were riding in the limo, Dash says, 'I love our family.' What changed their minds?" (Discovering how to use their superpowers for good, discovering a family mission, working together.)

WHAT SHOULD WE DO?

ASK: "What could we have as *our* family mission statement?"

TODAY'S SLOGAN: "Hope makes us heroes at home."

ADAPTING FOR . . .

YOUNGER CHILDREN: View the movie early enough in the day so you won't have sleepyheads at the end, or show it in two settings. If you have a children's picture storybook Bible, show pictures from some of the Old Testament stories (like Joshua), where people of God had to be strong and courageous (David and Goliath; Daniel and the lion's den, etc.).

TEENS: If your teen doesn't want to watch the entire movie, select ten minutes and watch that together, then extend the Discussion and ASK: "What are some ways teens need to be strong?" (Refer back to the Scripture.) "What are some ways teens can show they are courageous?"

PRAYER

Thank You God for our family. Thank You that we can work together and challenge evil and stand for what is good like the family did in the movie. Help us to stand together, even though it looks like the world is falling apart. In Jesus' name, Amen.

EXPERIENCE

•40• · Our Family Brand

MAIN POINT: We need to be clear and consistent about what's important.

MATERIALS: Paper, pen, construction paper, poster board, markers, scissors, tape, and glue. Optional: leather, canvas, wood, or ceramic clay.

WARM UP

ASK: "What is one rule that is really important in our family? Are we consistent with it? Why or why not? What might happen if this rule was only followed on Monday, Wednesday, and Friday?" **ASK:** "Sometimes a family is known for something. It might be a quality that sets them apart. They become known as being brave, kind, or generous. This becomes part of their identity—like a product's brand, families can have brands and be known for certain good things. What is our family known for?"

BIBLE READING: Read aloud Psalm 78:5–7:

He established a testimony in Jacob and appointed a law in Israel, which he commanded our fathers to teach to their children, that the next generation might know them, the children yet unborn, and arise and tell them to their children, so that they should set their hope in God and not forget the works of God, but keep his commandments. (ESV)

ASK: "What will you teach your grandchildren?"

FAMILY DISCUSSION

WHAT SHOULD WE DO?

1. ASK: "What is a quality or trait that has been passed along from grandma or grandpa and is being passed along to the kids in this family? (An appreciation for hard work; a love for homemade peach ice cream, etc.)

2. ASK: "What does the Bible reading say should be passed along from one generation to the next?" (Stories of God's miracles and His commands.)

3. ASK: "What happens if parents forget, or get too busy, to pass on their faith and love for God to their kids?" (The kids forget and stop following God.)

ACTIVITY: FAMILY CREST PROJECT

Search the Internet for images for "family crests" and "family shields." Look at several samples to get an idea of family crests. Make a family shield or crest based on today's Scripture. (If you already have a family Scripture, incorporate it.) Divide the crest into four parts to reflect your family's top four values (Example: Love, Working Together, Honor, Justice, etc.) Make the crest out of paper, leather, wood, or ceramics. You might integrate some of the themes and experiences from past Family Times. If you have time, develop a Family Mission statement (or motto) that incorporates your top values. You may choose to display your mission statement on your crest. If not, display it in another prominent place (like on the refrigerator). Display your family crest in a prominent place to remind family members of your *Family Mission.*

TODAY'S SLOGAN: "We want to pass along God's best."

ADAPTING FOR . . .

YOUNGER CHILDREN: ASK: "What is your favorite thing to do with mom or dad?" (If you can, make plans to do it as part of your Family Time or immediately after.) This illustrates the principle of taking the time for what matters most. Chances are, it is "pushing me in the swing," or "playing with me and my toys," so it won't take a huge amount of time.

TEENS: Enlist the teens in writing your Family Mission Statement (or motto) using the skills they have picked up from school. Keep it short, comprehensive, timeless, and memorable. Also, during the Discussion, **ASK:** "How can telling stories about what God has done give hope to kids and teens?"

PRAYER

Thank You God that You have given us a purpose as a family to be (review your values). By Your grace and strength, we will be this kind of family. In Jesus' name, amen.

•Part Three•

MILESTONES MOMENTS
RIGHTS OF PASSAGE
AND HOLIDAYS

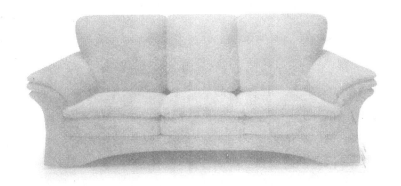

EXPERIENCE
·41·

Back to School

MAIN POINT: We should celebrate the joy of learning.

MATERIALS: Family car or transportation and time needed to visit a museum.

WARM UP

ASK: "What makes a person knowledgeable?" (He keeps on learning; he's teachable.) **ASK:** "Let's say we are on a family car trip and we get lost, what should we do?" (Stop and ask for directions from someone who lives there and knows their way around.)

BIBLE READING: Read aloud Proverbs 10:17:

> *The road to life is a disciplined life; ignore correction and you're lost for good. (MSG)*

WHAT DOES THE BIBLE SAY?

ASK: "How is life like a road?"

ACTIVITY: VISIT A MUSEUM

Focus on the joy of discovery and learning. Prepare your children to return to school by getting excited about what others have discovered, invented, or created (arts, cars, music, technology, etc.). This outing will take longer than the usual twenty minutes, but it will give you a nice break from the hubbub of shopping for back-to-school stuff, and it focuses on the real purpose of school—learning.

If you don't have a museum nearby, watch an educational show on PBS, the Discovery Channel, the History Channel, or the Travel Channel. Adapt the Discussion questions to fit.

FAMILY DISCUSSION

Consider packing a picnic lunch to eat at the museum. Many museums provide eating areas. During lunch . . .

1. **ASK:** "What was the most impressive thing you saw?"
2. **ASK:** "What showed a lot of discipline and hard work by the person who made the exhibit or art?"

WHAT SHOULD WE DO?

ASK: "What are some ways we can continue being life-long learners?" (Go to church, read the Bible, read books, visit museums, etc.)

TODAY'S SLOGAN: "Wise people are life-long learners."

ADAPTING FOR . . .

YOUNGER CHILDREN: Keep the museum visit short, probably around one hour and look for museums with activities and interactive exhibits for kids. Try a children's museum first.

TEENS: Make a list of three or more museums and let them select the one for the family to go to. It might be dedicated to cars or fashion, but go with it. Extend the Discussion and **ASK:** "Why does discovery and creation bring joy?" and "A fool is a person who thinks he knows it all and has lost the joy of discovery. How can we keep from being foolish and retain our joy of learning?"

PRAYER

Creator God, thank You for Your beautiful world You have made for us to enjoy. The blue skies, the sparkly stars, and the powerful ocean is simply a small piece of Your artistry. Help us to always be joyful about learning as an expression of our gratefulness to You. In Jesus' name, Amen.

EXPERIENCE
·42·

Halloween/
Harvest Season

MAIN POINT: We can be courageous.

MATERIALS: *Despicable Me* movie and popcorn.

WARM UP

ASK: "What does it mean to be courageous? Describe a story when the hero of a story, movie, or TV show was courageous? Share a time when you were courageous."

SCRIPTURE READING: Read aloud Deuteronomy 31:6:

> *Be strong and courageous. Do not fear or be in dread of them, for it is the LORD your God who goes with you. He will not leave you or forsake you. (ESV)*

WHAT DOES THE BIBLE SAY?

1. **SAY:** "Because the Lord will never leave us, we can be strong and courageous. The more we know about God and His Word, the better we know Him and it helps us to be courageous and not afraid. How does it help you to know God won't leave you?" Share a time when God gave you courage when you were afraid.

2. **SAY:** "In *Despicable Me* three orphan girls, Margo, Edith, and Agnes desperately wanted to be adopted and loved. They didn't want to be left in the orphanage. They didn't want to be alone."

ACTIVITY: *DESPICABLE ME* MOVIE

Watch the movie together.

FAMILY DISCUSSION

1. **SAY:** "Gru's goal was to be the *world's best bad guy*. He really didn't want to be a dad. He wanted to use Margo, Edith, and Agnes in his plot to steal the moon. But they changed his goal and his heart. What did you think of his ground rules: 'You will not touch anything. You will not cry. No annoying sounds . . .?'"

2. **ASK:** "Even though Gru was strange and didn't know how to be a dad, the girls were courageous and showed him what they needed and he changed. What are some ways compassion, joy, and love changed Gru?"

WHAT SHOULD WE DO?

1. **SAY:** "The Minions were mischievous in the beginning, but changed as Gru changed. What are some things they did to show kindness and love?"

2. **ASK:** "In this movie, we saw that evil can be overcome by good. In a way, we are all like orphans from Miss Hattie's Home for Girls. We fear being alone. We want to be adopted. We want to be loved. We want a home. We were spiritual orphans at one time, yet our Heavenly Father adopted us, gave us a home, gave us a name, and introduced us to brothers and sisters. In Christ, we have family—something we have all longed for. God will never leave us or abandon us. How does that make you feel?"

TODAY'S SLOGAN: "I am courageous because I'm not alone."

ADAPTING FOR . . .

YOUNGER CHILDREN: Don't watch the entire movie. Watch a few action scenes then discuss.

TEENS: Extend the Discussion and **ASK:** "Why is belonging so important to us? What happens to young people when they don't feel like they belong?"

PRAYER

Most Powerful God, You have the universe in Your palm. Nothing happens without You knowing about it. Help us place our trust in You and not be afraid. Amen.

EXPERIENCE

•43•

Thanksgiving

MAIN POINT: We thank God, for He is good.

MATERIALS: Copies of the responsive Bible reading (one per person), wooden yardstick, construction paper, key ring, scissors, string, markers, tape or glue, and drill.

WARM UP

ASK: "As we approach Thanksgiving, we have much to be thankful for. What are one or two things that each of you are thankful for?"

BIBLE READING: Read aloud Psalms 136:1–5, 25:

READ this responsively with the reader reading the first line and the rest of the family reading the *italicized* line.

Give thanks to the LORD, for He is good!
   His faithful love endures forever.
Give thanks to the God of gods.
   His faithful love endures forever.
Give thanks to the Lord of lords.
   His faithful love endures forever.
Give thanks to him who alone does mighty miracles.
   His faithful love endures forever.
Give thanks to him who made the heavens so skillfully.
   His faithful love endures forever.
He gives food to every living thing.
   His faithful love endures forever.

WHAT DOES THE BIBLE SAY?

ASK: "Why should we be thankful (grateful) to God?"

ACTIVITY: YARDSTICK MOBILE OF THANKS

Drill a hole one inch from each end of the wooden yardstick. Thread six feet of string through one end and tie it off. Thread the other end of the string through the center of a key ring and tie off at the end of the yardstick. This will create a basic mobile. You can tie another string to the key ring to hang your mobile. (All of this can be done in advance to save time during Family Time).

Gather the family and **SAY:** "We are going to create a mobile of thanks—to remind us that 'God is good, all the time.' We will display this at Thanksgiving. We have thirty-six inches on the yardstick, so we need thirty-six things we are grateful for. We have four family members, so we can each try to do about eight or nine *thanks hangings* out of construction paper. You can make them with words or symbols, or both." Hang the thirty-six *thanks hangings* about an inch apart, using string and tape.

OPTION: Have the parents take the first eight as a time-line for the early years: how we met, where we fell in love, our wedding, our first home, the first child, etc.

FAMILY DISCUSSION

WHAT SHOULD WE DO?

1. Beginning with the hanging from inch 1, **ASK:** someone to describe what they created as a *Thanks Hanging* and why.

2. After you have talked about each one, **SAY:** "Obviously, we have much to be thankful for in this family—past, present and future. How should we use our mobile for Thanksgiving? Where should we display it?"

TODAY'S SLOGAN: "God is good – all the time."

ADAPTING FOR . . .

YOUNGER CHILDREN: Help them with the cutting and gluing. You may have to **ASK:** "What are you thankful for?" and help them think of ways to illustrate it.

TEENS: You can provide more sophisticated supplies like borders, photos, clips from magazines, fancy trims, and graphics you can purchase at an art or scrapbook store. You can also suggest that each inch represents a year, beginning when dad and mom first met. This would project into the future things like, "Making the team; getting to drive; graduating from high school; being accepted to college, etc." This is thankfulness in the future—a form of grace and hope.

PRAYER

Hold the mobile in the air and mention a few items in your prayer: We are thankful for Your goodness to us: (mention a few *Thanks Hangings*) Father, as seen with all of these blessings on our mobile. Help us to remember that Your faithful love endures forever. Amen.

Christ-Centered Advent

MAIN POINT: Prepare your family for a Christ-centered Christmas.

MATERIALS: Large basket (or cardboard box), paper, and pen.

WARM UP

In early December, gather your family and **SAY:** "We are going to focus on Jesus this Christmas. We will focus on His love for others and learn from His example of *giving* rather than *getting*. Don't worry, we'll still have presents, we are just going to learn how to not get overwhelmed with the stuff and the busyness. What are some ways we can put Jesus first? What are some ways we can put others first?" (Record these in writing.) **SAY:** "When we put others first, however we do it, we are giving them a gift."

BIBLE READING: Read aloud Acts 20:35:

> *And I have been a constant example of how you can help those in need by working hard. You should remember the words of the Lord Jesus, "It is more blessed to give than to receive." (NLT)*

WHAT DOES THE BIBLE SAY?

ASK: "All the giving at Christmas can remind us of Christ's gift at that first Christmas. What is your favorite decoration that reminds us of Jesus' birth?" (Nativity scene, etc.) **ASK:** "How can it be more *blessed to give than to receive?*"

ACTIVITY: CHRISTMAS BASKET

Part of the lesson will affect your family's grocery shopping. Once a week in December, have *Soup Night.* Instead of a more expensive meal, you will have soup, and with the money you save, buy groceries to put in your *Christmas Basket.* Place the basket in a visible place and fill it with canned foods, candy canes, baking supplies, and other festive food items. You can decorate your basket with Christmas colors, ribbons, etc. As Christmas draws closer, ask family members to pray about and look for a particular family in financial need that would benefit from your Christmas basket. Depending on the relationship, you may want to visit as a family when you drop off the basket, or simply leave it at the family's front door as a surprise.

FAMILY DISCUSSION

WHAT SHOULD WE DO?

Each Soup Night, **ASK:** "How does it make you feel to give up a full meal for soup?" The basket is getting more and more stuff in it as Christmas gets closer. How does that make you feel? Have your friends noticed the basket? What did they say?"

TODAY'S SLOGAN: "It is more blessed to give than to receive."

ADAPTING FOR . . .

YOUNGER CHILDREN: Involve them in decorating the basket and explain to them how God uses us to meet the needs of others. You might consider adding a family-friendly movie to your Christmas basket for the whole family to enjoy. **ASK:** "What do you think the kids will do when they see this movie in the basket?"

TEENS: Develop a *Christmas Activity Plan* to help pace your family in the busy holiday season. **SAY:** "We want to plan a Christmas that is Christ-centered, relaxing and fun. We can't do everything. What would you say are the most important things to do?" Working with your teen, develop a plan that reflects your family's values and traditions. Ask your teen to present the draft plan and lead a discussion at the next Family Night. For example, your teen might want to skip caroling this Christmas and serve as a family at a charity.

PRAYER

Father God, You gave Your Son. We celebrate the birth of Jesus now. We are so grateful to You for being generous and giving us a gift that really fits—life forever with You. Thank you in Jesus' name. Amen.

EXPERIENCE

·45·

A Christmas Gathering

MAIN POINT: Christmas is about being close. God wanted us to be close to Him, so He sent His very best—Jesus.

MATERIALS: One personalized ornament for every family member, a candle, matches or lighter, shoebox, wrapping paper, scissors, ribbon, and Christmas cards from friends and family.

WARM UP

SAY: "Christmas is about celebrating Jesus and being together. We can't be with everyone we love. We send Christmas cards to remember and care about others. God's Christmas *card* was Jesus. What are some ways Jesus is like a Christmas card?" (He brings good news, He expresses love, He wants to be with us, etc.)

BIBLE READING: Read aloud John 8:12:

Again Jesus spoke to them, saying, "I am the light of the world. Whoever follows me will not walk in darkness, but will have the light of life." (ESV)

WHAT DOES THE BIBLE SAY?

1. **ASK:** "Christmas is full of lights, stars, and hope, pointing to Jesus as the light of the world. Why is light so important?"

2. **ASK:** "We decorate our tree with lights and ornaments. They help us remember certain events that happened in our family story and in the story of Christmas. What are some of our favorite ornaments? Why?"

ACTIVITIES: AFFIRMATION ORNAMENT

After Thanksgiving, start reflecting on the year's significant events for each family member: a notable achievement, a significant learning, a developing passion, skill, or character trait— really anything that represents that past year in their life; and look for an ornament that symbolically matches this quality, experience, or achievement. (Some parents keep notes and look for ornaments all year.) Mom and Dad are included and surprise each other with an ornament they select for each other. If you can't find one that fits, make one.

On Christmas Eve, light candles, dim the lights, and present each family member with their wrapped, personalized *Affirmation Ornament.* **SAY:** "This year you have made some wise choices, so we present you with this ornament." (A wise owl ornament.) Or, "You have learned to swim like a fish." (Dolphin ornament.) Or, "You graduated!" (A graduate ornament.) You can either hang the ornaments on the tree, or keep them separate so they are accessible to show others during the holidays.

After a few years of this tradition, imagine the stories as you decorate your tree, and your children re-live the significant events of their lives as they *hang their life*, one ornament at a time.

I first heard about this powerful tradition from Mark and Melissa Whaley of Conifer, CO. He wrote, "Since this is something my folks did with me, our kids all know my life story through my ornaments, and enjoy remembering the meaning behind all of their Dad's ornaments as well as their own. They also know all the stories behind the ornaments that Melissa and I have given to each other in our married life."

What a legacy! Reflection, affirmation, connection, and expression all add up to a family tradition of telling stories of light and hope at Christmas!

TWELVE DAYS OF CHRISTMAS CARDS

Wrap a shoebox with Christmas wrapping paper, and label it *Christmas Card Box*. As your Christmas cards arrive, place them in the box vertically, in the order they arrive. Starting December 12, and every day until Christmas, before meals, chose the card in the front of the box and pray for that family as you thank God for your food. Then, place the card at the back of the box. You may want to pray specifically for something mentioned in the card or letter.

FAMILY DISCUSSION

WHAT SHOULD WE DO?

After you pray for the family represented by their card, **ASK:** "What do you know about this family? Do you remember the last time we saw them?" And other similar questions.

TODAY'S SLOGAN: "Jesus is the Light of the world."

ADAPTATIONS FOR . . .

YOUNGER CHILDREN: Have the youngest child in the family make the *Christmas Card Prayer Box*. You may need to help with the cutting and gluing, but leave as much of it as possible to him. You may want to cut a hole in the top or remove the top.

TEENS: **ASK:** "What do you hope your ornament next Christmas will represent? What has been your favorite ornament over the years?"

PRAYER

Dear Father God, thank You for sending Your precious Son to be our sacrifice. We know You did this because You love us. You want us to be together—to be close. Help us to love and know You more this Christmas. In Jesus' name, Amen.

A Family New Year's Eve

MAIN POINT: God has provided for our needs and has given us a whole new year to remember Him and appreciate what He does for us.

MATERIALS: Food for a meal, candles, sparkling cider, plastic champagne glasses, dessert, gold ribbons, silver seal stickers, and parchment-looking paper.

ADVANCE PREPARATION: You will need to prepare a certificate for each child that commemorates *significant achievements* or *display of character this past year.* Use your computer to personalize each one, including the child's name in fancy font and printed on parchment-looking paper. (Examples: "Learned to Read," "Made a Great Friend," "Mastered the Fine Art of Bike Riding," "Showed Compassion to Others," "Made the Varsity Team.") You can also add gold ribbons and silver seal stickers to make it look official. (Available at office supply stores.)

WARM UP

Have a nice family dinner with candlelight and background music. At the meal, read the Scripture and **ASK:** "What are some ways we saw God work this past year? We don't want to forget those. How can we be sure to remember those?"

Read aloud Deuteronomy 8:10–16:

When you have eaten and are full, then you shall bless the LORD your God for the good land which He has given you. "Beware that you do not forget the LORD your God by not keeping His commandments, His judgments, and His statutes which I command you today, lest—when you have eaten and are full, and have built beautiful houses and dwell in them; and when your herds and your flocks multiply, and your silver and your gold are multiplied, and all that you have is multiplied; when your heart is lifted up, and you forget the LORD your God who brought you out of the land of Egypt, from the house of bondage; who led you through that great and terrible wilderness, in which were fiery serpents and scorpions and thirsty land where there was no water; who brought water for you out of the flinty rock; who fed you in the wilderness with manna, which your fathers did not know, that He might humble you and that He might test you, to do you good in the end." (NKJV)

FAMILY DISCUSSION

WHAT DOES THE BIBLE SAY?

1. **ASK:** "What does the passage say no one should forget, even when things are going great?"
2. **ASK:** "What does it mean to 'become so full of yourself and your things'?"
3. **ASK:** "As you look at the New Year—full of possibilities, accomplishments and growth; what are you excited about? What do you hope for? What do you think will happen?"

ACTIVITY: NEW YEAR'S EVE FAMILY PARTY

Set the clocks ahead two or three hours, and get ready to celebrate with the kids as the clock strikes *midnight.* Option: Serve chilled sparkling apple juice or cider in plastic champagne glasses and make a toast to each child as you present their certificates.

TODAY'S SLOGAN: "God has given us the gifts of time and each other."

ADAPTING FOR . . .

YOUNGER CHILDREN: Set the clocks so it will be *midnight* at eight p.m. Make an icon or a picture that illustrates your child's accomplishment on his certificate. You could also add an actual photo of him demonstrating his accomplishment (ex. riding his bike).

TEENS: Your teen may say something about the certificate being "cheesy," but she will keep it as proof that her parents love her and have acknowledged her growth. If you can, try to focus more on personal growth than academic or athletic achievement.

PRAYER

Dear Father God, we thank You for time—for the privilege of seeing all You did this past year. We look forward to the future with this brand new year where we can be alert to see You at work. We give You this day, our lives, and the year before us. Amen.

EXPERIENCE ·47·

Valentine's Day

MAIN POINT: We learn about love and faithfulness at home.

MATERIALS: Red or white wrapping paper, cardboard box with a lid, sixteen feet of ribbon, a small wrapped gift for each family member, construction paper (red or white), markers, and tape. (See the *Advance Preparation* section that follows.)

WARM UP *LOVE HEARTS*

Cut two to three inch hearts out of construction paper and with markers write something complimentary about each person in your family: "I love this about (name)." Make sure everyone has at least two or three love hearts. You might put these out a day ahead of time and have them begin early.

BIBLE READING: Read aloud John 15:13–15:

Greater love has no one than this, that someone lay down his life for his friends. You are my friends if you do what I command you. No longer do I call you servants, for the servant does not know what his master is doing; but I have called you friends, for all that I have heard from my Father I have made known to you. (ESV)

ADVANCE PREPARATION: Purchase the gifts, wrap them, wrap the box and lid separately—so the lid can be easily removed. Tie a ribbon to each gift and run the ribbon to each place setting. Place the ribbon under the plate. Replace the lid. Cover lid with love hearts.

ACTIVITY

Serve a meal that is related to Valentines: heart-shaped waffles or pancakes, cherry juice, strawberries, or bake cookies and use a heart-shaped cookie cutter. At the end of the meal, remove the lid to the box, and instruct each person (one at a time) to pull their ribbon and obtain their gift.

FAMILY DISCUSSION

WHAT SHOULD WE DO?

1. **ASK:** "What does the Bible say about the greatest kind of love?" (Be a servant.)
2. **ASK:** "How can you be a servant with our family? At school? On the team?"

TODAY'S SLOGAN: "Love is learned at home."

ADAPTING FOR . . .

YOUNGER CHILDREN: Assist her in writing or describing her *Love Heart*. She may need help in drawing what she loves, she can tell you and you can write it, or you can write it on a piece of paper and she can color to make it pretty. Help define and illustrate love and faithfulness to your child.

TEENS: Consider making the gift a nice surprise—a watch, iTunes Gift Card, a gift card for the movies or their favorite snack. For the Discussion, **ASK:** "What is the difference between friends and servants?" (The relationship is one of love not authority.) **ASK:** "What do true friends talk about?" (Everything.)

PRAYER

Dear Heavenly Father, help us to learn how to love and be faithful at home, with each other so that others might see Your love in us. Amen.

Palm Sunday

MAIN POINT: We celebrate Jesus, God's Son.

MATERIALS: Small clay pots, potting soil, a pony pack of flowers (connected plastic packs of small flowering plants), trowel, acrylic paints, brushes, purple ribbon, orange juice, 7-Up, juice glasses, and cut flowers or palm leaves.

WARM UP

ASK: "Have you seen those award shows when the celebrities arrive in big, fancy limousines and step out onto the red carpet wearing their finest clothes and jewelry? What is the purpose of the carpet and all of the attention?" (To show honor and value to someone who is important or famous.) "If a famous person visited your home, what would you do to make her/him feel welcome?"

BIBLE READING: Read aloud (at breakfast) Matthew 21:8–9:

Most of the crowd spread their cloaks on the road, and others cut branches from the trees and spread them on the road. And the crowds that went before him and that followed him were shouting, "Hosanna to the Son of David! Blessed is he who comes in the name of the Lord! Hosanna in the highest!" (ESV)

WHAT DOES THE BIBLE SAY?

ASK: "Why would people spread their coats and palm branches out?" (Because they want to honor Jesus and they didn't have red carpet in those days.)

ACTIVITY: PALM PARADE AND PLANTINGS

If you live in an area where you can get palm fronds get at least one per family member. (They are available at many florist shops or ask for a replica.) Rinse them outside and allow them to dry before bringing into the house. If palms aren't available, get a large bouquet of affordable cut flowers. Early on the Saturday before Palm Sunday, or on Palm Sunday, lay out the palms (or flowers) down the hall or into the kitchen. (With flowers, you will line a pathway to walk). For your Palm celebration, make *Praise Mimosa* out of orange juice and 7-Up. After breakfast, line everyone up to march and repeat, "Bless the One who comes in the name of the Lord!"

FAMILY DISCUSSION

1. **ASK:** "Why did Jesus show up on a donkey, with palm leaves instead of fancy carpet?" (He came to help people, not draw attention to himself.)

2. **ASK:** "Why didn't Jesus get the *red carpet treatment* when he made his arrival into Jerusalem?" (Red carpet wasn't available then.)

3. **ASK:** "Why did the people wave palms at Jesus as he rode in on the donkey?" (It was a way of showing honor and importance to someone; usually reserved for royalty. In a way, they were calling him a "prince" by calling him "Son of King David.")

4. **ASK:** "How do we show honor and respect to Jesus now?" (By putting Him first in our lives, by thinking *what would Jesus do* in this situation.)

TODAY'S SLOGAN: "Hallelujah! Jesus is Lord!"

ADAPTING FOR . . .

YOUNGER CHILDREN: Preschool kids will love the marching, especially if you can add some of their music to march to.

TEENS: Teens won't be into the marching and they will check to make sure the drapes are closed! So let them be cool and give them palm branches to wave up and down over their younger siblings. Make the parade shorter if you have older children and teens, or skip it all together and **ASK:** "What did you think about waking up to flowers and palm leaves on the floor?" (Expect, "I thought mom had gone crazy.")

PRAISE PLANTINGS (for teens and older children)
Make praise plantings out of the small clay pots by decorating them with art and slogans from today's Scripture. (Example: "Bless the One Who Comes in the Name of the Lord!") Use acrylic paints (or markers) for the decoration. When complete, place potting soil and one small flower from the pony pack in the pot. Clean off dirt and wrap with purple ribbon (representing the royalty of Jesus) and place in each bedroom as a reminder to think of Jesus' sacrifice during the Easter season.

PRAYER

Dear Jesus, You deserve our praise. You are our Savior, God's Son, the Prince of Peace, the Everlasting One, You alone are worthy of our worship. We celebrate You! Amen.

EXPERIENCE

·49·

Easter

MAIN POINT: Jesus still does miracles.

MATERIALS: Large river rocks (about the size of softballs up to the size of footballs; one per person) and markers.

WARM UP

SAY: "Today we will celebrate Jesus' victory over death. Because He is God's Son, He had power over death. The early Christians had a saying that they said in unison. Please repeat it after me, and then let's say it together: 'Christ has died.' (Repeat) 'Christ is risen.' (Repeat) 'Christ will come again.' (Repeat) Now together in unison, 'Christ has died. Christ is risen. Christ will come again.'" (Repeat)

BIBLE READING: Read aloud Matthew 28:1–7a:

Early on Sunday morning, as the new day was dawning, Mary Magdalene and the other Mary went out to visit the tomb. Suddenly there was a great earthquake! For an angel of the Lord came down from heaven, rolled aside the stone, and sat on it. His face shone like lightning, and his clothing was as white as snow. The guards shook with fear when they saw him, and they fell into a dead faint. Then the angel spoke to the women. "Don't be afraid!" he said. "I know you are looking for Jesus, who was crucified. He isn't here! He is risen from the dead, just as he said would happen. Come, see where his body was lying. And now, go quickly and tell his disciples that he has risen from the dead, and he is going ahead of you to Galilee. You will see him there. Remember what I have told you." (NLT)

FAMILY DISCUSSION

WHAT DOES THE BIBLE SAY?

ASK: "Why did God send the angel to roll the rock away?" (To let people see Jesus had risen.)

WHAT SHOULD WE DO?

ASK: "Just like God rolled the rock away, He wants to help us remove everything that keeps us from being with Jesus. What are some things that get in the way of being with Jesus?" (Too busy; not praying; forgetting to read the Bible; not thinking about Jesus when we are worshipping at church.)

ACTIVITY: ROCK 'N' ROLL

SAY: "Flowers, Easter eggs, bunnies, new clothes, baskets of candy and pastel colors are all part of Easter, but what about rocks? A huge rock was part of the very first Easter—the one the angel *rolled* away from the grave. So let's have a *rock'n'roll* Easter! We are going to make rocks that remind us of the resurrection miracle." **ASK:** "What were some of the miracles that Jesus did?" **SAY:** "We will now capture those miracle stories on rocks."

Have everyone take a river rock and decorate it with the markers—put symbols of God's power that help you remember stories in the Bible where the Lord did miracles. Also, write in large lettering a phrase from today's Scripture, or something related to the resurrection, like, "Don't be afraid! He isn't here. He is risen!"

TODAY'S SLOGANS: Traditional responsive Easter greeting: "Christ is risen!" (Response) "He has risen indeed!" Or, "Jesus rocks!"

ADAPTING FOR . . .

YOUNGER CHILDREN: Purchase smaller river rocks for your child and help them remember stories of Jesus doing miracles that they could illustrate on their rock. You may need to help him think of creative and simple ways to illustrate the story. (Example: Jesus fed thousands of people with a boy's sack lunch. Draw a sandwich and an apple.)

TEENS: Ask your teen to read 1 Corinthians 15:12–20 and **ASK:** "What would happen if Easter was just a fairy tale and Christ actually did not rise from the grave?" (We would have no hope and be miserable.)

PRAYER

Dear God, today we celebrate that Jesus rose from the dead and gives us new life. We celebrate that Your power still does miracles, just like that first Easter. Help us to look for Your power working in our lives. In the Risen Christ's name, Amen.

EXPERIENCE
•50•

Independence Day—July 4

MAIN POINT: Truth leads to freedom.

MATERIALS: Construction paper, scissors, markers, pencils, paper, clothes hanger, and fishing line.

WARM UP

ASK: "What is 'independence' and why do we celebrate it?" (Independence is the freedom of control of others. We celebrate our freedom from the rule of Great Britain when the Declaration of Independence was first adopted on July 4, 1776, and the United States of America was born.)

BIBLE READING: Read aloud John 8:32:

And you will know the truth, and the truth will set you free. (ESV)

WHAT DOES THE BIBLE SAY?

SAY: "If we know the truth, we will be free."

ACTIVITY: THE PLEDGE HUNT

Draw twelve five-point stars on construction paper (with pencil) and cut out with scissors. Make them at least two or three inches wide. Number them 1 to 12. Write the *Pledge of Allegiance* broken down into twelve phrases on the twelve stars:

1. I pledge
2. Allegiance

3. To the flag
4. Of the United States of America
5. And to the Republic
6. For which it stands
7. One nation
8. Under God
9. Indivisible
10. With liberty
11. And justice
12. For All

When the Freedom Stars are completed, collect them and hide them in the house or in the backyard. Make sure the kids don't see you hiding them. When they are hidden, come back to the kids and **SAY:** "We are going to look for freedom today. Freedom isn't easy; we have to work at it. We have to look for it, and when we discover it, we have to keep it. We are going on a scavenger hunt for twelve stars that spell out our Pledge of Allegiance."

FAMILY DISCUSSION

WHAT SHOULD WE DO?

After the hunt, gather the stars and arrange them in order. Then lead a discussion using the following—

Pledge of Allegiance	Meaning
"I pledge"	A pledge is a promise.
"Allegiance"	Means I will be loyal and faithful to *be on their side*.
"To the flag"	The flag is a symbol of the ideas that made our country.

Pledge of Allegiance	Meaning
"Of the United States of America"	We are many states, but we are One family—on the same team.
"And to the Republic"	Means everyone gets a vote.
"For which it stands"	The flag represents this.
"One nation"	Even though we are many states, we are **one** nation.
"Under God"	People came to this land to worship God the way they wanted to.
"Indivisible"	Cannot be divided even though we have had challenges and disagreements; we choose to stay together.
"With liberty"	We aren't prisoners of anyone. We have freedom.
"And justice"	Fairness. Everyone getting what is right.
"For All"	Democracy includes everyone equally. All have rights.

On the back of the stars, write the meaning. Then hang the stars with different lengths of fishing line from the hanger to make a *Freedom Star Mobile*. Display it where you will see it.

TODAY'S SLOGAN: Memorize a patriotic poem.

My Country's Flag ©2006
by Suzanne Smith

Flag of my country
Reminds me that I'm free,
Free to be me!

ADAPTING FOR . . .

YOUNGER CHILDREN: Draw the stars for your child and help with the cutting. Explain the concepts of the pledge in terms she can understand.

TEENS: Ask your teen to hide the Freedom Stars. For the Discussion, **ASK:** "What are some examples of two or three of the meanings?" (Example: "Give me an example of *allegiance*.")

PRAYER

Dear Father God, thank You for our country and the many blessings we enjoy: freedom, honor, the rights to vote and worship, and that everyone is valuable. Help us build our lives, our family, and our country on Your truth, because that will make us really free. In Jesus name, Amen.

EXPERIENCE ·51·

Mother's Day

MAIN POINT: Moms are our everyday heroes.

MATERIALS: Food for mom's favorite breakfast or lunch, flowers, balloons, helium (or helium-filled balloons), string, streamers, recorded music and player, posters, markers, tape, and construction paper.

WARM UP

SAY: "Today we are going to honor mom. We want her to feel special and loved. What are some ways we can do that?"

BIBLE READING: Read aloud Proverbs 31:28–29:

Her children stand and bless her. Her husband praises her. "There are many virtuous and capable women in the world, but you surpass them all!" (NLT)

WHAT DOES THE BIBLE SAY?

ASK: "What does it mean to 'bless' your mom?" (Say nice things about her and show her respect and honor, etc.)

ACTIVITY: PEP RALLY FOR MOM

Mothers do so much behind the scenes. Today is the day to make her the heroine! Serve her coffee or tea in bed (if this is for breakfast) along with some fresh fruit or croissant. If it's lunch, keep her in another part of the house while you prepare, so it will be a surprise. Have the kids help make the meal and set a fancy table with the china, cloth napkins, candles, fresh flowers, etc.

Inflate balloons with helium and tie them together with string to make an arch. Hang streamers from the balloon arch. Mom will go through these (as a football team does at the start of a game).

Make several cheer posters, like: **"#1 MOM", "You Rock Mom!"** or **"Hero of My Heart."** (You can also use butcher paper for this, if you have it.) Make megaphones out of construction paper by rolling them into ice cream cone shapes and taping them. Have each child decorate their megaphone by drawing pictures of what they appreciate about mom and writing words of honor on their megaphone. When you are ready, start the music and have one person retrieve mom. She is to walk through the arch as you cheer her with your megaphones and give her high-fives and pats on the back. Before the meal, have each child pray a short prayer about what they appreciate about their mom. During the meal, each child can read what he wrote on his megaphone, then present to mom as a gift. Conclude with dad or the oldest child saying something like, "You surpass them all!" Kids do the clean-up, of course!

FAMILY DISCUSSION

WHAT SHOULD WE DO?

The best time for this discussion might be before the pep rally.

1. **ASK:** "Why are we supposed to honor mom?" (God commands us to; she deserves it.)
2. **ASK:** "What can we do on Mothers' Day to really make it her day and not ours?"

TODAY'S SLOGAN: "Mom is our hero!"

ADAPTING FOR . . .

YOUNGER CHILDREN: Assist in making the megaphone and in drawing something they like about mom.

TEENS: Enlist your teen to play peppy parade music on his musical instrument instead of playing the recorded music as Mom runs through the honor gauntlet. Teens might be able to cook a hot breakfast or lunch for mom.

PRAYER

Dear God, we rejoice in the mom You gave us. Thank You for her love, her faithfulness, and the hard work she does for our family. Help her feel honored today. In Jesus' name, Amen.

EXPERIENCE

·52·

Father's Day

MAIN POINT: A Godly father is worthy of honor.

MATERIALS: Twelve small gifts for dad, paper bags, fabric tote, tape, marker, pen, pencil, and food for a barbeque or ice cream.

WARM UP

Let dad have some free time to lounge with his favorite beverage. During the preceding week, pull the kids aside and **ASK:** "What would make dad feel special and loved for Fathers' Day?" See if you can incorporate some of their ideas into the following session.

BIBLE READING: Read aloud Ephesians 6:1–3:

Children, obey your parents because you belong to the Lord, for this is the right thing to do. "Honor your father and mother." This is the first commandment with a promise; If you honor your father and mother, "things will go well for you, and you will have a long life on the earth." (NLT)

WHAT DOES THE BIBLE SAY?

ASK: "What does it mean to obey your parents?" (Do as they tell you or according to their rules.)

ACTIVITY: HUNTER & GATHERER

Men like to hunt and gather, so let's give dad a fun day of hunting outside! Purchase at least a dozen small gifts that dad will like (golf balls, gift card to the home improvement store, razors, aftershave, favorite gum or candy, iTunes gift card, gift card to his favorite restaurant, etc.) and wrap these in newspaper or brown sack paper. Number them and hide them in the backyard or in your neighborhood park. Keep a record of where you hide each one. Gather the family and **SAY:** "Dad, for Fathers' Day we are going hunting, so get ready to go." If he has some camouflage or blaze orange hunting clothing, ask him to wear it! Provide a bag or tote for him to place his "game" as he gathers it. Wrap it up with a barbeque or ice cream.

FAMILY DISCUSSION

WHAT SHOULD WE DO?

1. **ASK:** "What part of *Hunter & Gatherer* did you enjoy?"
2. **ASK:** "Why is it important for kids to honor and obey their dads? What would happen if they didn't?" (They'd get in trouble and maybe hurt themselves.)
3. **ASK:** "When you think of dad, what are you thankful for?

TODAY'S SLOGAN: "Dad deserves my respect."

ADAPTING FOR . . .

YOUNGER CHILDREN: Allow them to hide some of the gifts for dad, and they can play *Cold, Warm, Hot.* "Cold" if dad is far away from the gift. "Warm" if he is getting closer, and "Hot" if he's really close.

TEENS: In the discussion, **ASK:** "What is the link between honoring dad and living a long life? Why is there a relationship between the two?" (To keep kids from living foolish lives that will be shortened.) "What are some ways teens can honor their dad, other than Fathers' Day?"

PRAYER

Father God, we thank You for our dad. As we look at his life and his heart, we see You, our Heavenly Father. Help us to appreciate him and cooperate with him and give him the respect he deserves; especially today as we celebrate him. In Jesus' name, Amen.

Tale of
Two Families

I t was 9:17 p.m. on a Saturday and I was exhausted. I didn't
even work that day! I barbequed dinner, corralled the girls
to take their baths, read them some stories and eventually got
them to bed.

I plopped down on the couch and wondered where the day
went. A terrifying thought entered my mind: *I only have so many
Saturdays with our daughters! What am I doing with them?* It's not
like I had wasted the day, *or had I?* Earlier in the day, I watched
my favorite college football team play their rival, caught a little
of *Sportscenter* and a little bit of the Ohio State game. I did a
little yard work and the day was over!

Ever feel like someone is diabolically speeding up certain
days?

I reached for my phone and pulled up the calculator:
940—there are only 940 Saturdays between my daughter's birth
and her leaving for college! Nicole was ten. 524 Saturdays had
slipped away. I only had 416 Saturdays left! Brooke was seven—
365 Saturdays—*a whole year had disappeared!* I only had 575
Saturdays to make a difference.

(If you really want to freak yourself out, illustrate that on a
timeline!)

When our kids were little the days seemed to drag on, but the
years flew by. The older our girls got the busier their Saturdays
were with sports, friends, and activities. The same goes for
Sundays. During the week, we were all busy with work, school,
homework, practice, and driving them all over the place.

Then it hit me. *I just can't wait for Saturdays. I have to capture the fleeting moments each day. I need to turn those few minutes into memorable moments.*

Here's what I tell clients in my family coaching practice, "Imagine your child is eighteen and he is going out the door to college. His room is practically empty; there are no toys on the floor or dirty boxers in the hallway. The video game controllers are out of sight. No backpack hanging on the chair in the kitchen. No homework books on the kitchen table. Everything is neat, quiet and where it should be. Hold the thought for effect … now rewind to the present and glance around—not so neat and quiet, is it? But today's moments with our kids are limited and they are passing. Will you take advantage of those precious moments while you have them?"

That time-traveling technique puts things into perspective, doesn't it? The toys on the floor seem less annoying. The laundry can pile up. The dishes can wait. The DVR can record the game.

I don't know how to slow down time, but I do have some tips on how to maximize the limited time you have with your children, as those 416 Saturdays left go flying by!

E.P.I.C. MOMENTS

In the Introduction of the book, I introduced you to Len Sweet's acrostic on how to connect with our kid's generation: **E.P.I.C.**

I think this is an excellent guide on how to optimize time with our kids.

Experiential—Use your customized *Family Faith Plan* to capture those thirty-six impression points you have each week. Try for "small wins." Quick, informal connections that engage the senses and leverage the moment, turning a normal, natural event into an impressionable moment to express love, acceptance, confidence or for spiritual formation. Set aside five minutes on Sunday to plan how you can use your *Family Faith Plan* that week for informal impressions with your children. For example, your nine year-old son has basketball practice on Tuesdays, so on the way home from work on Monday, you pick up his favorite sports drink (Taste) at the store, where you also text him: "I'll be home in 5 min. Let's play 1 on 1. Winner gets the Gatorade." You play a quick game to ten. Award him the drink for beating you, and give him a high five (Touch) and some affirmation (Talk): "You played awesome! Good game son." Total elapsed time (including store run): fifteen to twenty minutes. You can do this!

Participatory—Spiritual formation is not something we do *to* our kids—it's something we do *with* our kids. Ask them what they would like to do with you to grow spiritually. Sometimes they have the best ideas. They tend to come up with ideas that are age-appropriate. You could say, "I have ten minutes until we have to pick up your sister from her soccer practice at the park. Do you want to go now so we have time for me to push you on the swings? Or play catch?" While playing, look for ways to talk, connect, observe, and if you have the opportunity, talk about faith. You aren't forcing it—you are simply creating space and time for it to happen. When there is margin in our lives, God can speak.

Image–rich—With the average American child spending seven to eight hours a day with his eyes glued to a screen, Gen iY has become very image-oriented. Look for ways to use art, décor, furnishings, videos, video games, websites, and landscaping to create visual stimuli that enhances conversation and musing about spiritual truths. We have a rock garden where we have collected smooth river rocks with dates, Scripture, promises, and symbols written on them as reminders of times God showed up. I can't help but reflect on His faithfulness every time I walk by it.

Sometimes low-tech, visual input is very powerful.

Connection—There are two types of connection—technological and relational. Our kids need both. Consider how you furnish your home: does it promote casual conversations or does the formality or clutter get in the way? I've seen some homes that look like museums and never lived in; too stuffy. I've seen other homes that are in such disarray that it's distracting to try to talk, if you can even find a clear place to sit down; too much stuff! Shoot for something between museum and a home that looks like a scene from *Hoarders*.

Think strategically about how to make connections while you fix a quick breakfast, when you sit down for dinner and how to connect after school in the car. **Design a one-on-one connection with each child.** Make it weekly, bi-weekly, or monthly. *Participate* with them in designing what they'd like to do. Nicole and I have gone to McDonald's once a week since she was little. (Don't judge me, this was before *Supersize Me!*) She played on the Playland equipment, we'd eat, and it was fun. When she got into middle school, she stopped the Playland stuff and we just talked. For Brooke, it was a weekly sporting activity: surfing, running, basketball, or volleyball. She didn't want to just talk and eat—she wanted to be active.

Technology can keep you connected—or it can keep you from connecting with your child. *Use the force wisely Luke Skywalker.* I enjoy connecting with our daughters via text, email, and *Facebook*. On occasion, we go *old school* and actually talk on the phone! When I'm travelling I use it to "Check In" at places I'm visiting or eating and send them a photo. It keeps us connected and there's usually humor involved. It's easy for them to text: "LOL-hey pray 4 me ruf day @ work." They are grown and I'm way past my 940 Saturdays, but since I invested some random minutes here and there I'm reaping a relationship that is EPIC!

THREE KINDS OF EPIC MOMENTS

The first kind of EPIC moment is the *informal* moment when you can make a quick impression (like those you plan on your *Family Faith Plan*).

The second kind is the *intentional* moment that may be longer and scheduled. The first forty of the 52 Family Times are an example of those. Time that you are purposefully setting aside to set up faith talks and experiences.

The third type of EPIC moments are the *milestones* and holidays that provide a rite of passage or a season to generate conversations and thought about faith. (The last twelve of the 52 Family Times.) When a child goes through a transition like starting kindergarten or middle school, he is open for affirmation, information, and conversations about growing up and "the next step." It's a perfect time to work in faith talks. Don't just buy your child gifts for these milestones, leverage the milestones for spiritual significance by giving your child EPIC moments with you that foster his faith.

MAKING FAITH STICK

Peanut Butter Faith—was our topic in the opening pages. How can we make faith stick at home? I'd like to offer seven easy ways to make faith stick with your children and teens. These can easily be seen in *The Shema*. They are also discussed in a best-selling business book by brothers Chip Heath and Dan Heath, ***Made To Stick**—Why Some Ideas Survive and Others Die* (New York: Random House, Inc. 2008. 16-18).

1. **Simplicity**—For ideas to stick they need to be simple and profound. It's not about dumbing down; it's about removing the clutter and the complexity.
2. **Unexpectedness**—Children are born with wonder in their hearts. Introduce them to a God of wonder, miracles, and

surprises. Keep some mystery in your faith lest it become a ritual.

3. **Concreteness**—Lectures usually don't work with kids because they are too long and too abstract. Think of Proverbs—short, pithy sayings that carry a punch because they are timeless and concrete. Be clear. Be concise. And you'll be memorable.

4. **Credibility**—If parents first impress God's Word and His commandments on their own hearts before they try impressing them on their children's, they will have credibility with their children. Appealing to your authority doesn't enhance your credibility with kids, but being authentic does.

5. **Emotions**—People care about ideas when they have some emotion attached to them. Think about the "crazy" fans who paint their faces with their team colors and stand out in the cold for hours to cheer them on. They are emotional about their team winning! Share your passion with your kids. If you have a passion for God, they are likely to catch it.

6. **Stories**—People act on ideas when they hear stories; especially when they feel that in some way they are part of the story. Stories put content into a framework that is more lifelike, more like our common, everyday experience. Oral tradition has been a powerful tool to pass on culture, values, and inspiration. Stories inspire people to act.

Chip Heath and Dan Heath offer these six elements to make ideas stick. It is an acrostic:

S.U.C.C.E.S

And they build the structure of their book around it. I like the book and I was thinking that *The Shema* has all of these, and more: it's Simple—"as you walk along the way."

It's Unexpected—"tie theme to your head." It's Concrete—
"These commandments—the ten I just gave you." It's
Credible—ah, it came from God. It's Emotional—"write these
on our hearts." It's based on Stories—the story of God's love
being passed on from generation to generation. But there's one
element that is in *The Shema* that isn't in **Made To Stick**. And it's
too bad because it makes the spelling accurate: S.U.C.C.E.S.**S.**

Spirit—dependent. We can have the first six elements of
The Shema as discussed in **Made to Stick**, but without the Spirit
of God working we won't have lasting faith. God's Spirit com-
municates when we can't. His Spirit comforts when we can't.
The Holy Spirit convicts our kids when we don't even know they
have sinned.

To have sticky faith and to have SUCCESS in making an
impression of vital faith on our children, we absolutely must
depend on the Spirit of God. No formulas or programs work
quite like the Spirit of God!

Ask God to prompt you when to speak and when to not
speak with your child. Listen to Him. Depend on Him. That's
what I do. I often remind myself that I need self-control or kindness and those don't come easy for me, but they are fruit of the
Holy Spirit (Galatians 5:22).

TWO FAMILY LEGACIES

You have in your hand the tools to rewrite your story. You may
have come from a family of brokenness, addiction, dysfunction,
and hypocritical faith. But with God's grace, you can rewrite the
next chapter for you and your children. It's a choice you make
every day with the small, seemingly insignificant decisions you
make. Will you weave in faith or will you keep it in a tidy box
reserved for church? Will you lead your family in faith talks or
will you outsource that to the children's ministry?

The whole point of *The Shema* is so that our children and grandchildren don't forget God, His promises and His commandments. We love the story of Joshua. Against all odds and opposition, he depends on God and fights through for success. Joshua ends with "But as for me and my household, we will serve the Lord!" (Joshua 24:15 NIV). It sounds like a scene from *Braveheart* with Mel Gibson boldly declaring with booming voice across the valley "But as for me and my household, we will serve the Lord!" Followed by thunderous applause. We like this verse so much that many of us have it posted in our homes.

But there is a second family story—one that isn't so cheery, or made for Hollywood. Judges paints with darker strokes (2:10) "After the whole generation had been gathered to their fathers, another generation grew up who knew neither the Lord nor what He had done for Israel." (NIV)

What happened? What changed from a few pages ago with Joshua?

The fathers had stopped telling the stories. (Deuteronomy 8:11)

The mothers had stopped weaving in faith with their nurture.

A generation died without impressing on their children the mighty acts and character of God.

We have to keep telling the story. We have to be storytellers of the faithfulness of God, in good times and in challenging situations.

We must write these commandments on our own hearts, and then get them inside the hearts of our kids and grandkids.

Which of these two family stories will be your legacy with your family?

THE END

©Timothy Smith

52+ CREATIVE FAMILY TIME EXPERIENCES

Here's a tip from one of the dads from the four hundred plus families that field-tested these ideas before the book was published. He handed me a list and said, "At my engineering job, we always make a *materials list*. So I made one for your book. You can gather all of the materials; then when it's time to do Family Time, you are ready to go. Here's what needs to go in the box."

I suggest that you get a cardboard box and decorate it with your children. Write "Family Time Stuff" on the outside and stock it with basic materials. That way you'll have most of what you need for most sessions ready to go. You will just need to get a few things for that particular session. Your basic stock includes: construction paper, scissors, tape, markers, string, yarn, butcher paper, poster board, pencils, pens, drawing paper, candles, balloons, and popcorn.

The following shows the session number and what you will need for that session.

SESSION	MATERIALS
1	Socks, bowls, and string
2	A ball of yarn
3	Broomstick, twine, tape, and paper
4	Twelve small river stones and permanent markers
5	Popcorn and *Finding Nemo* movie
6	Park with playground equipment, toy blocks or dominoes

SESSION	MATERIALS
7	Construction paper, scissors, markers, and tape
8	Baby food, spoon, juice, sipper cup, and bib
9	Butcher paper, scissors, and markers
10	Dictionary, a can of peaches, spoons, bowls and can opener
11	Popcorn and *Up* movie
12	Paper and pen
13	Car to drive to store
14	Fake check, butcher paper, pencils, rulers, crayons, and markers
15	Clear glass jar, walnut-sized rocks, marbles, sand, bowls, and masking tape
16	Tape measure, painter's tape, chalk, broomstick, recorded music and music player
17	Wood blocks or books, bubble soap and wands, pie tin, flex ties, and pipe cleaners
18	Play dress-up clothes, player, recorded music, pen and paper
19	Popcorn and *The Blindside* movie, newspaper, blindfold, and trashcan
20	Neighborhood park
21	Cotton balls, tape, candy, purse, bathrobe, and broomstick
22	Shoeboxes, construction paper, glue, old magazines, and scraps of fabric

SESSION	MATERIALS
23	Shoelaces (or twine)
24	A sturdy kitchen chair
25	A bucket, washcloths, towel, water, soap, chair, and perfume
26	Popcorn, with two bowls, and *Toy Story* movie
27	Construction paper, tape, and markers
28	Sack lunch supplies, cookie ingredients, grocery cash card
29	Battery-powered toy or tool, nutrition bars, and sports drinks
30	Individually wrapped candies, ice cream scoop, large bowl, and blindfold
31	One dollar and a dime for each family member, pen, and paper
32	Drawing paper, markers, shoebox, brown or black construction paper; glue, rope ,bangles & knick-knacks to decorate with and balsa wood strips (optional)
33	Popcorn, *Shrek 2* movie, old magazines and scissors
34	Pen, paper, plastic grocery bags, clear contact paper, crayons, scissors, and nature stuff (leaves, sticks, etc.)
35	Ten pennies per child, a muffin tin, masking tape, marker, pen, and paper. **OPTIONAL:** cupcakes as a treat

SESSION	MATERIALS
36	Popcorn and *Soul Surfer* movie
37	Two small Ziploc® bags, a wire coat hanger, masking tape, pen, and fifty pennies
38	Twine (or yarn), chair, and scissors
39	Popcorn and *The Incredibles* movie
40	Paper, pen, construction paper, poster board, markers, scissors, tape, and glue. **OPTIONAL:** leather, canvas, wood, or ceramic clay
41	Family car, nearby museum
42	Popcorn and *Despicable Me* movie
43	Copies of Bible reading, wooden yardstick, construction paper, key ring, scissors, string, markers, tape, and drill
44	Large basket (or cardboard box), paper, and pen
45	Personalized ornament for each family member, candle, matches, shoebox, wrapping paper, ribbon, and Christmas cards from friends
46	Food for a meal, candles, sparkling cider, plastic champagne glasses, dessert, gold ribbons, silver seal stickers, and parchment-looking paper

SESSION	MATERIALS
47	Red or white wrapping paper, cardboard box with a lid, sixteen feet of ribbon, a small wrapped gift for each family member, construction paper (red or white), markers, and tape. **Advance preparation needed**
48	Small clay pots, potting soil, a pony pack of flowers, trowel, acrylic paints and brushes, purple ribbon, orange juice, 7UP, juice glasses, and cut flowers or palm leaves
49	Large river rocks (at least softball size) and markers
50	Construction paper, scissors, markers, pencils, paper, coat hanger, and fishing line
51	Food for breakfast or lunch, flowers, balloons, helium, string, streamers, recorded music and player, posters, markers, tape, and construction paper
52	Twelve small gifts for dad, paper bags, tape, marker, pen, pencil, and food for barbeque or ice cream

Appendix

For More Ideas on Creative Family Times, check out the following websites:

WWW.D6FAMILY.COM/607
Digital interactive family worship resource for churches

WWW.PARENTSCOACH.ORG
Parenting tips, videos, blogs, speaking calendar for the author

WWW.D6FAMILY.COM
Resources, info about the D6 conference, videos, etc.

WWW.FAITHATHOME.COM
Mark Holmen's site with resources, videos, and blogs

WWW.HOMEWORD.COM
An extensive site with tons of content and FAQs for parents

WWW.FAMILYMATTERS.NET
Dr. Tim Kimmel offers regular dinner table discussions

WWW.STRONGFAMILIES.COM
Dr. John Trent's site for strong marriages and families

WWW.FOCUSONYOURCHILD.COM
Focus on the Family's site for parents

WWW.FAMTIME.COM
Learn how to have family times with trainer Kirk Weaver

If you have some ideas or stories you'd like to share about your Family Time, let us know at **WWW.PARENTSCOACH.ORG**

Endnotes

[1] Dr. Tim Elmore, *Generation iY–Our Last Chance to Save Their Future* (Atlanta, Poet Gardner Publishing, 2010) 49.

[2] Dr. Kara E. Powell & Dr. Chap Clark, *Sticky Faith–Everyday Ideas to Build Lasting Faith in Your Kids* (Grand Rapids, MI, Zondervan, 2011).

[3] Christian Smith with Melinda Lundquist Denton, *Soul Searching; The Religious and Spiritual Lives of American Teenagers* (New York: Oxford Press, 2005) 56.

[4] "Soul Searching" panel discussion from March 2008, available at http:fulleryouthinstitute.org/2008/03/soul-searching-panel/.

[5] Leonard Sweet, *Post-Modern Pilgrims: First Century Passion for the 21ˢᵗ Century World* (Nashville: Broadman and Holman, 2000).

Join the conversation with other families about their creative family time experiences at
WWW.CREATIVEFAMILYTIMES.COM

Visit the author at **WWW.PARENTCOACH.ORG**
to find out more about his coaching, speaking and resources.

I NEED YOU TO LEAD ME.

Also Available in Kindle, Nook™ and iPad™

THE LEGACY PATH

Discover Intentional Spiritual Parenting

BRIAN HAYNES

AN INTENTIONAL PLAN TO EMPOWER YOU TO LEAD YOUR CHILDREN TO SPIRITUAL MATURITY.

Available at **Amazon.com**
Group discounts available at **D6Family.com** or **800-877-7030**

legacypathbook.com

by randall house ⓗ

D6 Devotional Magazines
for the entire family!

D6 Devotional Magazines are unique because they are the only brand of devotional magazines where the entire family studies the same Bible theme at the same time.

Think about how long it would take you to track down all of the resources for each member of your family to connect with God on the same topic. Who has that kind of time? We do! It's not that we have nothing else to do, we are just passionate about D6. So look no further, we have created the resource for which you are looking, and it works!

D6 Devotional Magazines are full-color, interactive, fun, and exciting tools to connect with God and with each other.

Subscribe now!
800.877.7030
D6family.com

EVERY MARRIAGE
MATTERS TO GOD.

After years of counseling engaged and married couples, the Rienows realized that most Christian couples didn't know WHY God had brought them together! *Visionary Marriage* will reveal that God does have a plan and a purpose for marriage and family in the Bible. The focus is on the big-picture purpose for marriage, and the goal of being successful once understanding the purpose.

Ideal for small group study with discussion questions at the end of each chapter.

Visionary Marriage by Rob and Amy Rienow $12.99
Group discounts available